Cambridge Latin Course

Book II

FOURTH EDITION

CAMBRIDGE
UNIVERSITY PRESS

University Printing House, Cambridge CB2 8BS, United Kingdom

Cambridge University Press is part of the University of Cambridge.

It furthers the University's mission by disseminating knowledge in the pursuit of education, learning and research at the highest international levels of excellence.

Information on this title: education.cambridge.org

This book, an outcome of work jointly commissioned by the Schools Council before its closure and the Cambridge School Classics Project, is published under the aegis of Qualifications and Curriculum Authority Enterprises Limited, Newcombe House, 45 Notting Hill Gate, London W11 3JB.

First published 1971
Second edition 1982
Integrated edition 1990
Fourth edition 2000
22nd printing 2016

Printed in Poland by Opolgraf

A catalogue record for this publication is available from the British Library.

ISBN 978-0-521-64468-6 Paperback

Cover photographs: front: cat © British Museum; mosaic © Roger Dalladay; back © Roger Dalladay
Maps and plans by Neil Stanton / Eikon Illustration
Illustrations by Joy Mellor and Leslie Jones

ACKNOWLEDGEMENTS
Thanks are due to the following for permission to reproduce photographs:
p. 1, G. Soffe; p. 5 *r*, by permission of the National Museum of Wales; p. 5 *l*, p.16 *t*, Cambridge University Museum of Archaeology and Anthropology; p. 11, p. 33, St. Albans Museums; p. 17 *t*, Dr. Simon James, *c*, *b*, © Estate of Alan Sorrell / English Heritage Photographic Library; p. 19 *t*, *br*, p. 20, p. 22, p. 37 *t*, *bc*, p. 39 *br*, p. 41 *tl*, *2nd from top + bottom r*, p. 62 *l*, p. 75, p. 81 *l*, *c*, p. 82 *c*, p. 86 *c*, p. 89 *l*, p. 103 *t*, *b*, p. 116 *l*, p. 127 *tr*, p. 129 *tl*, p. 130, p. 131 , p. 139, p. 141, p. 142 *b*, p. 143 *b*, p. 144 *tr*, *tl*, *bl* © The British Museum; p. 19 *bl*, Dr P.J. Reynolds / Butser Ancient Farm; p. 23, p. 25, p. 39 *tr*, © The Museum of London; p. 38 *c*, p. 42, Colchester Museums; p. 39 *l*, *cr*, Colchester Archaeological Trust; p. 54, Bob Croxford / Atmosphere; p. 57 *t*, *br*, Francesca Radcliffe, *bl*, The Society of Antiquaries of London; p. 58, Dorchester County Museum; p. 56 *b*, p. 59, p. 69, p. 70 *tc*, *bl*, p. 71 *cr*, p. 72 *r*, p. 74, Fishbourne Roman Palace / Sussex Archaeological Society; p. 67, John Deakin; p. 82 *r*, p. 114 *l*, Don Flear; p. 84–5, p. 88 *t*, Jean-Claude Golvin, *Le Phare d'Alexandrie*, coll. Découvertes Gallimard, © Editions Gallimard Jeunesse; p. 86, *b*, George Hart; p. 88 *b*, p. 91 *t*, *bl*, Stephane Compoint, Sygma; p. 90, © IFAO / Alain Leclerc; p. 97 *r*, © Photo RMN / Richard Lambert; p. 105 *b*, p. 106 *t*, p. 107 *l*, *r*, The Corning Museum of Glass, New York State; p. 115, Württembergisches Landesmuseum Stuttgart, Frankenstein, Zweitasch; p. 117 *r*, The National Gallery; p. 127 *b*, Michael Holford; p. 129 *b*, Archiv Alinari, Firenze; p. 145, © Photo RMN / H. Lewandowski / Musée du Louvre

Other photography by R.L. Dalladay. Thanks are due to the following for permission to reproduce photographs:
p. 6 Dr Gerald Brodribb / Beauport Park; p. 9, p. 114 *r*, p. 137, Bardo Museum, Tunis; p. 13, p. 26, p. 56 *c*, p. 62 *c*, *r*, Landesmuseum, Trier; p. 31, p. 34, p. 36 *t*, p. 40 *r*, p. 56 *c*, p. 81 *r*, p. 82 *l*, p. 86 *t*, p. 97 *l*, p. 105 *t*, p. 107 *b*, p. 111, p. 117 *3rd l*, p. 126 *c*, *r*, British Museum; p. 36 *c*, *b*, p. 41 *bl*, *tr*, p. 57 *inset*, p. 70 *tr*, p. 92, p. 109 *t*, p. 122, p. 123 *r*, p. 124, p. 126 *l*, p. 128, p. 129 *tr*, p. 147, Museo Archeologico Nazionale, Naples; p. 37 *br*, Musei Capitolini, Rome; p. 56 *t*, Sousse Museum; p. 100, p. 110, p. 123 *l*, Museo Nazionale Romano, Rome; p. 116 *2nd l*, *3rd l*, *4th l*, Musée du Louvre, Paris; p. 117 *2nd l*, Pushkin Museum, Moscow; p. 120, p. 127 *tl*, Sperlonga Site Museum; p. 133 , Monumenti Musei e Gallerie Pontificie, Vatican City.

Every effort has been made to reach copyright holders. The publishers would be glad to hear from anyone whose rights they have unknowingly infringed.

Contents

IN BRITANNIA

STAGE 13

1 hic vir est Gāius Salvius Līberālis.
   Salvius in vīllā magnificā habitat.
   vīlla est in Britanniā.
   Salvius multōs servōs habet.

2 uxor est Rūfilla.
   Rūfilla multās ancillās habet.
   ancillae in vīllā labōrant.

3 hic servus est Vārica.
   Vārica est vīlicus.
   vīlicus vīllam et servōs cūrat.

4 hic servus est Philus.
Philus callidus est.
Philus numerāre potest.

5 hic servus est Volūbilis.
Volūbilis coquus optimus est.
Volūbilis cēnam optimam coquere
potest.

6 hic servus est Bregāns.
Bregāns nōn callidus est. Bregāns
numerāre nōn potest.
Bregāns fessus est.
Bregāns dormīre vult.

7 hic servus est Loquāx.
Loquāx vōcem suāvem habet.
Loquāx suāviter cantāre potest.

8 hic servus est Anti-Loquāx.
Anti-Loquāx agilis est.
Anti-Loquāx optimē saltāre potest.
Loquāx et Anti-Loquāx sunt geminī.

9 Salvius multōs servōs habet. servī
labōrant.
servī ignāvī et fessī sunt.
servī labōrāre nōlunt.

trēs servī

trēs servī in vīllā labōrant. haec vīlla est in Britanniā. servī dīligenter labōrant, quod dominum exspectant. servī vītam suam dēplōrant.

Philus: *(pecūniam numerat.)* iterum pluit! semper pluit! nōs sōlem numquam vidēmus. ego ad Ītaliam redīre volō. ego sōlem vidēre volō. 5

Volūbilis: *(cēnam in culīnā parat.)* ubi est vīnum? nūllum vīnum videō. quis hausit? ego aquam bibere nōn possum! aqua est foeda!

Bregāns: *(pavīmentum lavat.)* ego labōrāre nōlō! fessus sum. multum vīnum bibī. ego dormīre volō. 10

(Vārica subitō vīllam intrat. Vārica est vīlicus.)

Vārica: servī! dominus noster īrātus advenit! apud Canticōs servī coniūrātiōnem fēcērunt. dominus est vulnerātus.

Bregāns: nōs dē hāc coniūrātiōne audīre volumus. rem nārrā! 15

Britanniā: Britannia	*Britain*
dēplōrant: dēplōrāre	*complain about*
pluit	*it is raining*
sōlem: sōl	*sun*
Ītaliam: Ītalia	*Italy*
redīre volō	*I want to return*
aquam: aqua	*water*
bibere nōn possum	*I cannot drink*
foeda	*foul, filthy*
pavīmentum	*floor*
lavat: lavāre	*wash*
labōrāre nōlō	*I do not want to work*
fessus	*tired*
advenit: advenīre	*arrive*
apud Canticōs	*among the Cantici*
coniūrātiōnem: coniūrātiō	*plot*
vulnerātus	*wounded*

Sometimes slaves were kept in chains. Here is a neck-chain for slaves which was found in East Anglia.

A neck-chain from Wales being worn by volunteers.

Clues to a Roman mine

Salvius had visited the Cantici to inspect an iron mine. The site of one of these mines has been found near Hastings.

Quantities of slag (waste from extracting the iron) have been found at the site. In the 19th century 100,000 tonnes of it were removed from the site and used for road building.

Top: *Rusty water at the site shows that there is iron in the ground.*

Left: *The stamp on a tile shows that the mine was run by the Roman fleet (CLBR stands for classis Britannica).*

coniūrātiō

Vārica rem nārrāvit:

'nōs apud Canticōs erāmus, quod Salvius metallum novum vīsitābat. hospes erat Pompēius Optātus, vir benignus. in metallō labōrābant multī servī. quamquam servī multum ferrum ē terrā effodiēbant, Salvius nōn erat contentus. Salvius servōs ad 5 sē vocāvit et īnspexit. ūnus servus aeger erat. Salvius servum aegrum ē turbā trāxit et clāmāvit,

"servus aeger est inūtilis. ego servōs inūtilēs retinēre nōlō." postquam hoc dīxit, Salvius carnificibus servum trādidit. carnificēs eum statim interfēcērunt. • 10

•hic servus tamen fīlium habēbat; nōmen erat Alātor. Alātor patrem suum vindicāre voluit. itaque, ubi cēterī dormiēbant, Alātor pugiōnem cēpit. postquam custōdēs ēlūsit, cubiculum intrāvit. in hōc cubiculō Salvius dormiēbat. tum Alātor dominum nostrum petīvit et vulnerāvit. dominus noster erat 15 perterritus; manūs ad servum extendit et veniam petīvit. custōdēs tamen sonōs audīvērunt. in cubiculum ruērunt et Alātōrem interfēcērunt. tum Salvius saeviēbat. statim Pompēium excitāvit et īrātus clāmāvit, •

"servus mē vulnerāvit! coniūrātiō est! omnēs servī sunt 20 cōnsciī. ego omnibus supplicium poscō!"

Pompēius, postquam hoc audīvit, erat attonitus.

"ego omnēs servōs interficere nōn possum. ūnus tē vulnerāvit. ūnus igitur est nocēns, cēterī innocentēs."

"custōdēs nōn sunt innocentēs", inquit Salvius. "cum Alātōre 25 coniūrābant."

Pompēius invītus cōnsēnsit et carnificibus omnēs custōdēs trādidit.'

metallum *a mine*
hospes *host*
quamquam *although*
ferrum *iron*
effodiēbant: effodere *dig*
ad sē *to him*

inūtilis *useless*
carnificibus: carnifex
   executioner

nōmen *name*
vindicāre voluit
   wanted to avenge
itaque *and so*
ubi *when*
cēterī *the others*
pugiōnem: pugiō *dagger*
custōdēs: custōs *guard*
ēlūsit: ēlūdere *slip past*
manūs ... extendit *stretched
   out his hands*
veniam petīvit
   begged for mercy
saeviēbat: saevīre *be in a rage*
cōnsciī: cōnscius *accomplice*
supplicium *death penalty*
poscō: poscere *demand*
nocēns *guilty*
innocentēs: innocēns *innocent*
coniūrābant: coniūrāre *plot*
invītus *unwilling, reluctant*

Bregāns

When you have read this story, answer the questions on page 9.

tum Vārica, postquam hanc rem nārrāvit, clāmāvit,
 'Loquāx! Anti-Loquāx! dominus advenit. vocāte servōs in
āream! ego eōs īnspicere volō.'
 servī ad āream celeriter cucurrērunt, quod Salvium timēbant.
servī in ōrdinēs longōs sē īnstrūxērunt. vīlicus per ōrdinēs   5
ambulābat; servōs īnspiciēbat et numerābat. subitō exclāmāvit,
 'ubi sunt ancillae? nūllās ancillās videō.'
 'ancillae dominō nostrō cubiculum parant', respondit Loquāx.
 'ubi est Volūbilis noster?' inquit Vārica. 'ego Volūbilem vidēre
nōn possum.'   10
 'Volūbilis venīre nōn potest, quod cēnam parat', respondit
Anti-Loquāx.
 Bregāns in mediīs servīs stābat; canem ingentem sēcum
habēbat.
 'ecce, Vārica! rēx Cogidubnus dominō nostrō hunc canem   15
mīsit', inquit Bregāns. 'canis ferōcissimus est; bēstiās optimē
agitāre potest.'
 subitō vīgintī equitēs āream intrāvērunt. prīmus erat Salvius.
postquam ex equō dēscendit, Vāricam salūtāvit.
 'servōs īnspicere volō', inquit Salvius. tum Salvius et Vārica 20
per ōrdinēs ambulābant.
 puerī puellaeque in prīmō ōrdine stābant et dominum suum
salūtābant. cum puerīs stābant geminī.
 'salvē, domine!' inquit Loquāx.
 'salvē, domine!' inquit Anti-Loquāx.   25
 Bregāns, simulac Salvium vīdit, 'domine! domine!' clāmāvit.
Salvius servō nihil respondit. Bregāns iterum clāmāvit,
 'Salvī! Salvī! spectā canem!'
 Salvius saeviēbat, quod servus erat īnsolēns.
 'servus īnsolentissimus es', inquit Salvius. Bregantem ferōciter 30
pulsāvit. Bregāns ad terram dēcidit. canis statim ex ōrdine
ērūpit, et Salvium petīvit. nōnnūllī servī ex ōrdinibus ērūpērunt
canemque retrāxērunt. Salvius, postquam sē recēpit, gladium
dēstrīnxit.
 'istum canem interficere volō', inquit Salvius.   35
 'illud difficile est', inquit Bregāns. 'rēx Cogidubnus, amīcus
tuus, tibi canem dedit.'
 'ita vērō, difficile est', respondit Salvius. 'sed ego tē pūnīre
possum. illud facile est, quod servus meus es.'

in āream *into the courtyard*

in ōrdinēs *in rows*
sē īnstrūxērunt: sē īnstruere
 draw oneself up
per ōrdinēs *along the rows*

sēcum *with him*

rēx *king*

equitēs: eques *horseman*
equō: equus *horse*

puerī puellaeque
 the boys and girls
geminī *twins*

simulac *as soon as*

īnsolēns *rude, insolent*
ērūpit: ērumpere *break*
 away
nōnnūllī *some, several*
retrāxērunt: retrahere
 drag back
sē recēpit: sē recipere
 recover
illud *that*
pūnīre *punish*
facile *easy*

Questions

Marks

1 Why did Varica want to inspect the slaves? What did he tell the twins to do (lines 2–3)? 2
2 In line 4 which two Latin words show that the slaves were in a hurry? Why did they hurry? 2
3 In lines 8–12 why were the slave-girls and Volubilis missing from the inspection? 2
4 **canem ingentem sēcum habēbat** (lines 13–14). How did Bregans come to have the dog with him? What did he say about the dog (lines 15–17)? 1 + 2
5 Salvius is an important Roman official. How do lines 18–19 show this? Give two details. 2
6 How did Salvius react in lines 27 and 29 when Bregans called out to him? Why do you think Salvius called Bregans **īnsolentissimus** (line 30)? 2 + 1
7 What happened to Bregans after Salvius hit him? 1
8 How did the dog nearly cause a disaster (lines 31–2)? 2
9 Who saved the situation? What did they do? 1 + 2
10 **Salvius...gladium dēstrīnxit** (lines 33–4). What did Salvius want to do? Why did he change his mind? 2
11 **ego tē pūnīre possum** (lines 38–9). Did Bregans deserve to be punished? Give a reason. 1
12 Which two words from this list do you think best describe Bregans in this story: brave, stupid, impetuous, cheeky? Give reasons for your choice. 2

TOTAL **25**

STAGE 13 9

About the language 1: infinitives

1   Study the following pairs of sentences:

        Loquāx cantat.   Loquāx **cantāre** vult.
        Loquax is singing.   *Loquax wants **to sing**.*

        servī dominum vident.   servī dominum **vidēre** nōlunt.
        The slaves see the master.   *The slaves do not want **to see** the master.*

        puerī currunt.   puerī celeriter **currere** possunt.
        The boys are running.   *The boys are able **to run** quickly.*

        Salvius Bregantem pūnit.   Salvius Bregantem **pūnīre** potest.
        Salvius punishes Bregans.   *Salvius is able **to punish** Bregans.*

    The form of the verb in bold type is known as the infinitive. It usually
    ends in **-re** and means 'to do (something)'.

2   Translate the following examples and write down the Latin infinitive
    in each sentence:

    a   Anti-Loquāx currit. Anti-Loquāx currere potest.
    b   Bregāns labōrat. Bregāns labōrāre nōn vult.
    c   geminī fābulam audīre volunt.
    d   senēs festīnāre nōn possunt.

3   The verbs **volō**, **nōlō** and **possum** are often used with an infinitive.
    They form their present tense as follows:

(ego)	volō	*I want*	(ego)	nōlō	*I do not want*
(tū)	vīs	*you (singular) want*	(tū)	nōn vīs	*you (singular) do not want*
	vult	*s/he wants*			
(nōs)	volumus	*we want*		nōn vult	*s/he does not want*
(vōs)	vultis	*you (plural) want*	(nōs)	nōlumus	*we do not want*
	volunt	*they want*	(vōs)	nōn vultis	*you (plural) do not want*
				nōlunt	*they do not want*

(ego)	possum	*I am able*
(tū)	potes	*you (singular) are able*
	potest	*s/he is able*
(nōs)	possumus	*we are able*
(vōs)	potestis	*you (plural) are able*
	possunt	*they are able*

4 **possum**, **potes**, etc. can also be translated as 'I can, you can', etc.:

nōs dormīre nōn possumus.   *We are not able to sleep* or *We cannot sleep.*
ego leōnem interficere possum.   *I am able to kill the lion* or *I can kill the lion.*

5 Further examples:

    a   ego pugnāre possum.
    b   nōs effugere nōn possumus.
    c   tū labōrāre nōn vīs.
    d   coquus cēnam optimam parāre potest.
    e   celeriter currere potestis.
    f   in vīllā manēre nōlō.
    g   labōrāre nōlunt.
    h   vīnum bibere volumus.

British hunting dogs were prized all over the world. One is shown here on a Romano-British cup made near Peterborough.

Salvius fundum īnspicit

postrīdiē Salvius fundum īnspicere voluit. Vārica igitur eum per
fundum dūxit. vīlicus dominō agrōs et segetem ostendit.
    'seges est optima, domine', inquit Vārica. 'servī multum
frūmentum in horreum iam intulērunt.'
    Salvius, postquam agrōs circumspectāvit, Vāricae dīxit,   5
'ubi sunt arātōrēs et magister? nōnne Cervīx arātōribus
praeest?'
    'ita vērō, domine!' respondit Vārica. 'sed arātōrēs hodiē nōn
labōrant, quod Cervīx abest. aeger est.'
    Salvius eī respondit, 'quid dīxistī? aeger est? ego servum   10
aegrum retinēre nōlō.'
    'sed Cervīx perītissimus est', exclāmāvit vīlicus. 'Cervīx sōlus
rem rūsticam cūrāre potest.'
    'tacē!' inquit Salvius. 'eum vēndere volō.'
    simulatque hoc dīxit, duōs servōs vīdit. servī ad horreum   15
festīnābant.
    'quid faciunt hī servī?' rogāvit Salvius.
    'hī servī arātōribus cibum ferunt, domine. placetne tibi?'
respondit Vārica.
    'mihi nōn placet!' inquit Salvius. 'ego servīs ignāvīs nūllum   20
cibum dō.'
    tum dominus et vīlicus ad horreum advēnērunt. prope
horreum Salvius aedificium vīdit. aedificium erat sēmirutum.
    'quid est hoc aedificium?' inquit Salvius.
    'horreum novum est, domine!' respondit vīlicus. 'alterum   25
iam plēnum est. ego igitur horreum novum aedificāre voluī.'
    'sed cūr sēmirutum est?' inquit Salvius.
    Vārica respondit, 'ubi servī horreum aedificābant, domine,
rēs dīra accidit. taurus, animal ferōx, impetum in hoc aedificium
fēcit. mūrōs dēlēvit et servōs terruit.'   30
    'quis taurum dūcēbat?' inquit Salvius. 'quis erat neglegēns?'
    'Bregāns!'
    'ēheu!' inquit Salvius. 'ego Britannīs nōn crēdō. omnēs
Britannī sunt stultī, sed iste Bregāns est stultior quam cēterī!'

agrōs: ager *field*
segetem: seges *crop, harvest*
frūmentum *grain*
horreum *barn, granary*
intulērunt: īnferre *bring in*
arātōrēs: arātor *ploughman*
magister *foreman*
nōnne? *surely?*
praeest: praeesse
    be in charge of
eī *to him*
perītissimus: perītus *skilful*
sōlus *alone, only*
rem rūsticam *the farming*
cūrāre *look after, supervise*
simulatque *as soon as*
hī *these*
ferunt: ferre *bring*
ignāvīs: ignāvus *lazy*

aedificium *building*

dīra *dreadful*

taurus *bull*
animal *animal*
impetum: impetus *attack*
neglegēns *careless*
Britannīs: Britannī *Britons*

This wall-painting from Roman Gaul shows a master coming to inspect his villa.

About the language 2: -que

1   In this Stage, you have met a new way of saying 'and' in Latin:

        puerī puellae**que**   *boys and girls*
        dominus servī**que**   *master and slaves*

    Note that **-que** is added on to the end of the second word.

    Rewrite the following examples using **-que** and translate them.

    a   servī et ancillae
    b   agricolae et mercātōrēs

2   **-que** can also be used to link sentences together:

        dominus ex equō dēscendit vīllam**que** intrāvit.
        The master got off his horse and went into the house.

        custōdēs in cubiculum ruērunt servum**que** interfēcērunt.
        The guards rushed into the bedroom and killed the slave.

3   Further examples:

    a   Vārica servōs ancillāsque īnspexit.
    b   Bregāns canisque in ōrdine stābant.
    c   Salvius āream intrāvit Vāricamque salūtāvit.
    d   Volūbilis ad culīnam revēnit cibumque parāvit.
    e   taurus impetum fēcit mūrōsque dēlēvit.

Practising the language

1 Complete each sentence of this exercise with the most suitable infinitive from the box below. Then translate the whole sentence. Do not use any infinitive more than once.

īnspicere	dormīre
numerāre	labōrāre
manēre	bibere

a Philus est callidus. Philus pecūniam . . . . potest.
b Loquāx et Anti-Loquāx sunt fessī. puerī . . . . volunt.
c Salvius est dominus. Salvius servōs et fundum . . . . vult.
d Cervīx est aeger. Cervīx . . . . nōn potest.
e Volūbilis laetus nōn est. Volūbilis aquam . . . . nōn vult.
f servī contentī nōn sunt. servī in vīllā . . . . nōlunt.

2 Complete each sentence with the right form of the noun. Then translate the sentence.

a . . . . in fundō labōrābat. (agricola, agricolae)
b . . . . fūrem nōn vīdērunt. (custōs, custōdēs)
c . . . . epistulās longās scrībēbant. (servus, servī)
d cūr . . . . prope iānuam lātrābat? (canis, canēs)
e . . . . , quod multam pecūniam habēbat, vīllam magnificam aedificāvit. (senex, senēs)
f . . . . , postquam in forō convēnērunt, ad tabernam contendērunt. (amīcus, amīcī)

3 Fill in the gaps in this story with the most suitable verb from the box below, and then translate the whole story. Do not use any word more than once.

cōnspexī	pulsāvī	vituperāvī	obdormīvī	fūgī
cōnspexistī	pulsāvistī	vituperāvistī	obdormīvistī	fūgistī
cōnspexit	pulsāvit	vituperāvit	obdormīvit	fūgit

servus in cubiculō labōrābat. servus, quod erat fessus, in cubiculō
. . . .

    Salvius, postquam cubiculum intrāvit, servum . . . . ; statim
fūstem cēpit et servum . . . .

    Rūfilla, quod clāmōrēs audīvit, in cubiculum ruit.

Rūfilla: tū es dominus pessimus! cūr tū servum . . . . ?
Salvius: ego servum . . . . , quod in cubiculō dormiēbat.
Rūfilla: herī tū ancillam meam . . . . , quod neglegēns erat.
           ancilla perterrita erat, et ē vīllā . . . .
Salvius: in vīllā meā ego sum dominus. ego ancillam . . . . ,
           quod ignāva erat.

Britannia

'… the spine-chilling sea and the Britons at the very end of the earth.'

Catullus

'The population of the island is countless. Houses rather like those in Gaul are to be seen everywhere and there are enormous numbers of cattle. They use either bronze or gold coinage.'

Julius Caesar

Bronze and enamel ornament from a horse harness, showing the artistry of British craftsmen.

Although the Romans thought of Britannia as a strange and distant land at the very edge of the known world, the island had its own highly developed civilisation before the Romans arrived. We know from archaeological evidence that the Britons were very good metalworkers, carpenters, weavers and farmers. Romans writing about the Britons, however, did not usually acknowledge their achievements.

Farms in Roman Britain

Most inhabitants of Roman Britain lived in the countryside. A typical small farm belonging to a native Briton would have provided for the basic needs of the farmer and his family and their slaves, with perhaps a little surplus left over for trade. His

A British farmhouse was circular, thereby minimising heat loss through the walls, which were usually made of wattle and daub attached to a wooden frame. The steeply sloping thatched roof allowed rain and snow to run off quickly.

Wattle and daub: basketwork covered with clay.

house consisted of a single round room where everyone in the family lived, worked, slept and ate. Since there were no windows, and only one low, narrow doorway, most of the light would have been provided by the open fire in the centre of the room, which also served as a place to cook and as a source of heat. Without a chimney the room must have been quite smoky inside.

About thirty years after the Roman invasion in AD 43, simple villas began to appear in the countryside. They had only four or five rooms, sometimes linked by a corridor; they were built mainly of timber and wattle and daub, with roofs of stone slabs, tiles or thatch. Some of these early villas are found on the sites of British roundhouses. It is likely that the Britons were attempting to imitate the lifestyle of their Roman conquerors and thus win their favour. Although the owners would have greater privacy and comfort in their new villa, it would have been more difficult and expensive to heat. These early villas are very similar to those found in Roman Gaul. The Britons may have learnt the new building techniques required from Gallic builders and craftsmen.

Later villas were often more complicated in design and were built mostly of stone; the grandest ones might contain long colonnades, under-floor heating, an ornamental garden, mosaics, and a set of baths complete with tepidarium and caldarium. They also had workshops, barns, living quarters for the farm labourers and sheds for the animals. In choosing a place to build his villa, the owner would look not only for attractive surroundings but also practical advantages, such as a nearby supply of running water and shelter from the cold north and east winds.

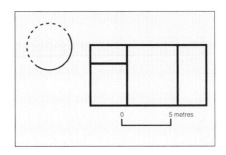

0   5 metres

Plan of an early villa built beside a former roundhouse at Brixworth in Northamptonshire.

Reconstruction of a later villa in Lullingstone, Kent.

The economy of the farm

The main crops grown in Britain at this time were barley, oats, rye and especially wheat. Archaeologists have found seeds of all these crops, accidentally charred and thus preserved in the earth. Most farms seem to have kept animals such as cattle, sheep, goats, pigs, dogs and horses, in addition to geese and hens; not only did these animals provide food, wool or leather clothing, fertiliser and bone tools, but they could also be used for transport or to provide security. Bees were kept to produce honey, which was used to sweeten food (there was no sugar at that time). Many fruits and vegetables were grown, including some (like cherries and peas) which had been brought to Britain by the Romans. The villas could not produce everything they needed, but home-made products such as leather, meat, timber and honey could be traded for shellfish, salt, wine, pottery and ironware.

A large villa like that belonging to Salvius would be supervised by a farm manager or bailiff. He was often a slave like Varica. The bailiff was responsible for buying any food or other goods that could not be produced on the villa's own land, and for looking after the buildings and slaves. In his book *On agriculture*, the Roman writer Columella says that the bailiff should be middle-aged and toughened from childhood by farm work.

Pre-Roman Britons probably had sheep like the Soay (above). *During the Roman period a breed like the Shetland* (below) *was developed.*

A reconstruction of an early villa in Britain. How many different farming activities can you see?

Roman bronze model ploughman, with a yoke of oxen.

Emmer, one of the kinds of wheat the Romans grew. It is bearded like barley .

A pre-Roman British gold coin showing a similar ear of wheat. CAMV stands for Camulodunum (Colchester) where the coin was minted.

The slaves

Farm slaves were described by one Roman landowner as just 'farming equipment with voices'. Most of Salvius' farm slaves would be British, whereas many of his skilled house slaves would be imported from abroad. Slaves working on the land lived a much harsher life than domestic slaves, and slaves working in the mines had the harshest life of all. Many of these had been sent to work in the mines as a punishment and conditions were so bad that this amounted to a death sentence. Some slaves were kept in chains.

In theory, the law gave slaves some protection: for example, any owner who killed a sick slave could be charged with murder. In practice, these laws were often ignored, as in the story of Salvius and the Cantican miners. However, in the first century AD slaves were becoming increasingly scarce and expensive; owners therefore had more motivation to look after the welfare of their slaves.

Some British slaves are known to us by name. For example, a gravestone from Chester was set up by a master in memory of three of his slaves who died young: a slave-boy aged twelve and two ten-year-olds called Atilianus and Anti-Atilianus, probably twins.

A weary young slave-boy waits with a lantern to light his master's way home.

Salvius

Gaius Salvius Liberalis was born in central Italy but, like many ambitious and clever young men, he soon moved to Rome, where he gained a reputation for speaking his mind. After becoming a successful lawyer, he was made a Roman senator, probably by the Emperor Vespasian. In AD 78, at a very early age, he was chosen as one of the Arval brotherhood, a group of twelve distinguished men who met to perform religious ceremonies and in particular to pray for the emperor and his family. Salvius was also put in command of a legion; not only was this a great honour, but it also showed the trust in which Salvius was held by Vespasian. Not long afterwards, in about AD 81, he was sent by Titus, the next emperor, to help Agricola, the Roman governor of the province of Britain.

Salvius' main task was probably to supervise the law courts and look after the southern part of the province while Agricola was away fighting in the north. He would have travelled around the country acting as a judge; he may also have arranged for some of the money raised by farming and mining in Britain to be sent regularly to the emperor in Rome. The stories set in Roman Britain imagine Salvius and his wife Rufilla living in an impressive villa not far from Noviomagus (Chichester) near the Sussex coast.

Our knowledge of Salvius comes mainly from the details on a commemorative stone discovered in central Italy and an inscription found in a wood near Rome. He is also mentioned by two Roman writers, Pliny and Suetonius. Another gravestone has been found dedicated by his son:

To Vitellia Rufilla, daughter of Gaius, wife of Gaius Salvius Liberalis the consul, priestess of the welfare of the Emperor, best of mothers, Gaius Salvius Vitellianus set this up in his lifetime.

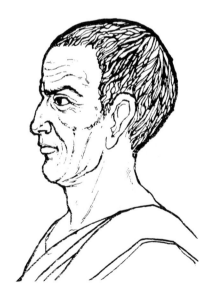

An artist's impression of Salvius. How closely does it fit your idea of his character?

Vocabulary checklist 13

The way verbs are listed in the checklists for Stages 13–16 is explained on p. 171.

adveniō, advenīre, advēnī	arrive	**ita vērō**	yes
aedificium	building	**nōlō**	I do not want
aeger	sick, ill	**novus**	new
alter	the other, the second	**nūllus**	not any, no
		possum	I can, I am able
cantō, cantāre, cantāvī	sing	**ruō, ruere, ruī**	rush
cēterī	the others, the rest	**sē**	himself
		trahō, trahere, trāxī	drag
custōs	guard	**vīta**	life
dīcō, dīcere, dīxī	say	**volō**	I want
excitō, excitāre, excitāvī	arouse, wake up	**vulnerō, vulnerāre, vulnerāvī**	wound
fessus	tired		
interficiō, interficere, interfēcī	kill		

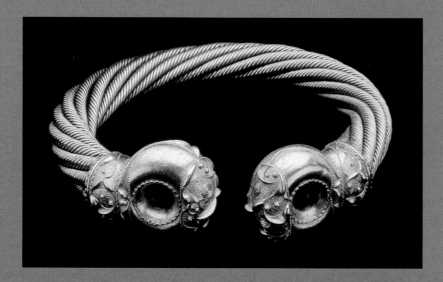

This spectacular gold torc (neck-ornament) was made about 70 BC, presumably for a British chieftain.

APUD SALVIUM

STAGE 14

1 Vārica: Phile! portā hanc amphoram
            in vīllam!
   Philus: amphora magna est. difficile
            est mihi magnam amphoram
            portāre.
   Vārica: cūr?
   Philus: quod ego sum senex.

2 Vārica: Loquāx! Anti-Loquāx!
            portāte hanc amphoram in
            vīllam!
   Loquāx: amphora gravis est. difficile
            est nōbīs amphoram gravem
            portāre.
   Vārica: cūr?
   Loquāx: quod nōs sumus puerī.

3 Vārica: Bregāns! portā hās
            amphorās in vīllam!
   Bregāns: amphorae gravēs sunt.
            difficile est mihi amphorās
            gravēs portāre.
   Vārica: sed necesse est!
   Bregāns: cūr?
   Vārica: necesse est tibi amphorās
            portāre quod Philus est
            senex, quod Loquāx et frāter
            sunt puerī, et…
   Bregāns: quod tū es vīlicus!

Rūfilla

Rūfilla in cubiculō sedet. duae ōrnātrīcēs prope eam stant et crīnēs compōnunt. Salvius intrat. Rūfilla, simulatque eum cōnspicit, ōrnātrīcēs ē cubiculō dīmittit.

Rūfilla:	Salvī! vir crūdēlis es. ego ad hanc vīllam venīre nōlēbam. in urbe Londiniō manēre volēbam. Londinium est urbs pulcherrima, ubi multās amīcās habeō. difficile est mihi amīcās relinquere.
Salvius:	Rūfilla! quam levis es! ubi in urbe Londiniō habitābāmus, cotīdiē ad mē veniēbās. cotīdiē mihi dīcēbās, 'ego quoque vīllam rūsticam habēre volō, sed tū mihi nihil dās.' tandem vīllam tibi dedī, sed etiam nunc nōn es contenta.
Rūfilla:	sed ego vīllam prope urbem habēre volēbam. haec vīlla ab urbe longē abest.
Salvius:	tū ipsa eam ēlēgistī. ego, quamquam pretium magnum erat, eam libenter ēmī. nōnne haec vīlla est ēlegāns? nōnne etiam magnifica?
Rūfilla:	sed hiems iam appropinquat. nōn commodum est mihi in vīllā rūsticā hiemāre. amīcae meae semper in urbe hiemant. in hōc locō sōla sum. amīcās meās vīsitāre nōn possum.
Salvius:	quid dīxistī? sōla es? decem ancillās habēs, novem servōs, duās ōrnātrīcēs, coquum Aegyptium…
Rūfilla:	et marītum crūdēlissimum. nihil intellegis! nihil cūrās! *(exit lacrimāns.)*

ōrnātrīcēs: ōrnātrīx *hairdresser*

dīmittit: dīmittere *send away, dismiss*
crūdēlis *cruel*
5 **Londiniō: Londinium** *London*
amīcās: amīca *friend*
relinquere *leave*
levis *changeable, inconsistent*

10 **vīllam rūsticam: vīlla rūstica** *house in the country*
etiam *even*

ab urbe *from the city*
15 **tū ipsa** *you yourself*
pretium *price*
libenter *gladly*
ēlegāns *tasteful, elegant*
hiems *winter*
20 **appropinquat: appropinquāre** *approach*
commodum: commodus *convenient*
hiemāre *spend the winter*
25 **novem** *nine*
lacrimāns *weeping, crying*

A comb and manicure set from Roman London.

A lady with four ōrnātrīcēs.

Domitilla cubiculum parat

I

'Domitilla! Domitilla! ubi es?' clāmāvit Marcia. Marcia anus erat.
  'in hortō sum, Marcia. quid vīs?' respondit Domitilla.
  'necesse est nōbīs cubiculum parāre', inquit Marcia. 'domina familiārem ad vīllam invītāvit.'
  'ēheu!' inquit Domitilla. 'fessa sum, quod diū labōrāvī.'   5
  'puella ignāvissima es', inquit Marcia. 'domina ipsa mē ad tē mīsit. necesse est tibi cubiculum verrere. necesse est mihi pavīmentum lavāre. curre ad culīnam! quaere scōpās!'
  Domitilla ad culīnam lentē ambulābat. īrāta erat, quod cubiculum verrere nōlēbat.   10
  'ego ōrnātrīx sum', inquit. 'nōn decōrum est ōrnātrīcibus cubiculum verrere.'
  subitō Domitilla cōnsilium cēpit et ad culīnam quam celerrimē festīnāvit. simulac culīnam intrāvit, lacrimīs sē trādidit.
  Volūbilis attonitus, 'mea columba', inquit, 'cūr lacrimās?'   15
  'lacrimō quod miserrima sum', ancilla coquō respondit. 'per tōtum diem labōrāvī. quam fessa sum! nunc necesse est mihi cubiculum parāre. nōn diūtius labōrāre possum.'

anus *old woman*
quid vīs? *what do you want?*
necesse *necessary*
familiārem: familiāris
  relation, relative
diū *for a long time*
domina ipsa
  the mistress herself
verrere *sweep*
scōpās: scōpae *broom*
lentē *slowly*
decōrum: decōrus *right, proper*

lacrimīs sē trādidit
  burst into tears
miserrima
  very miserable, very sad
diūtius *any longer*

'mea columba, nōlī lacrimāre!' inquit Volūbilis. 'ego tibi
cubiculum parāre possum.'

    'Volūbilis! quam benignus es!' susurrāvit ancilla.

    coquus cum ancillā ad cubiculum revēnit. dīligenter labōrāvit
et cubiculum fēcit pūrum. ancilla laeta

    'meum mel!' inquit. 'meae dēliciae!' et coquō ōsculum dedit.

    coquus ērubēscēns ad culīnam revēnit.

20

25

nōlī lacrimāre *don't cry*	
pūrum: pūrus *clean, spotless*	
mel *honey*	
ōsculum *kiss*	
ērubēscēns *blushing*	

II

tum Marcia cubiculum intrāvit. anus vix prōcēdere poterat,
quod urnam gravem portābat. Domitilla, ubi Marciam
cōnspexit, clāmāvit,

    'ecce! dīligenter labōrāvī. cubiculum fēcī pūrum. nunc necesse
est tibi pavīmentum lavāre.'

    Marcia, quamquam erat attonita, Domitillae nihil dīxit. sōla
pavīmentum lavābat. tandem rem cōnfēcit.

    Domitilla statim ad Rūfillam festīnāvit.

    'domina', inquit, 'cubiculum tibi parāvimus, et pavīmentum
fēcimus nitidum.'

    Rūfilla cubiculum cum Domitillā intrāvit et circumspectāvit.

    'bene labōrāvistis, ancillae', inquit. 'sed, quamquam nitidum
est pavīmentum, nōn decōrum est familiārī meō in hōc cubiculō
dormīre. nam cubiculum est inēlegāns. necesse est nōbīs id
ōrnāre.'

    'tablīnum est ēlegāns', inquit Domitilla. 'in tablīnō, ubi
dominus labōrat, sunt multae rēs pretiōsae.'

    'ita vērō', inquit Rūfilla, 'in tablīnō est armārium
ēlegantissimum. in tablīnō sunt sella aēnea et candēlābrum
aureum. age! Domitilla, necesse est nōbīs ad tablīnum īre.'

5

10

15

20

vix *hardly, scarcely*	
urnam: urna *bucket*	
sōla *alone, on her own*	
nitidum: nitidus *gleaming, brilliant*	
bene *well*	
nam *for*	
inēlegāns *unattractive*	
id *it*	
ōrnāre *decorate*	
armārium *chest, cupboard*	
aēnea *made of bronze*	
candēlābrum *lamp-stand, candelabrum*	
aureum: aureus *golden, made of gold*	
age! *come on!*	
īre *go*	

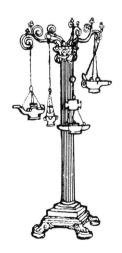
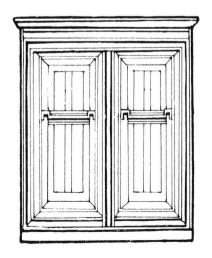

About the language 1: adjectives

1   Study the following sentences:

servus **stultus** nōn labōrābat.	*The **stupid** slave was not working.*
agricola servum **ignāvum** pūnīvit.	*The farmer punished the **lazy** slave.*
dominus servō **fessō** praemium dedit.	*The master gave a reward to the **tired** slave.*

The words in **bold type** are adjectives. They are used to describe nouns. In each of these examples, the adjective is describing the slave.

2   Adjectives change their endings to match the case of the noun they describe.
In the first sentence above, **stultus** is nominative because it describes a nominative noun (**servus**).
In the second sentence, **ignāvum** is accusative, because it describes an accusative noun (**servum**).
In the third sentence, **fessō** is dative, because it describes a dative noun (**servō**).

3   Translate the following examples:

a   ancilla perterrita ad culīnam contendit.
b   coquus ancillam perterritam salūtāvit.
c   cīvēs mercātōrem fortem laudāvērunt.
d   cīvēs mercātōrī fortī praemium dedērunt.
e   senex fīlium bonum habēbat.
f   senex fīliō bonō vīllam ēmit.

Write down the Latin noun and adjective pair in each sentence and state whether it is nominative, accusative or dative.

4 Adjectives also change their endings to match the number (i.e. singular or plural) of the nouns they describe. An adjective is singular if it describes a singular noun, and plural if it describes a plural noun. Compare the following examples with those in paragraph 1:

servī **stultī** nōn labōrābant.	*The stupid slaves were not working.*
agricola servōs **ignāvōs** pūnīvit.	*The farmer punished the lazy slaves.*
dominus servīs **fessīs** praemium dedit.	*The master gave a reward to the tired slaves.*

5 Translate the following examples:

  a fēminae laetae per viās ambulābant.
  b fēmina laeta per viās ambulābat.
  c gladiātor leōnēs ferōcēs necāvit.
  d coquus servīs aegrīs cibum parāvit.
  e pictūra pulchra erat in ātriō.
  f Volūbilis ōrnātrīcem trīstem cōnspexit.

Write down the Latin noun and adjective pair in each sentence and state whether the pair is singular or plural.

6 When an adjective changes its ending in this way it is said to *agree*, in case and number, with the noun it describes.

7 Most adjectives come after the noun. However, adjectives like **magnus**, **parvus** and **multī**, which indicate size or quantity, usually come before the noun they describe. For example:

  Rūfilla multās ancillās habēbat.   *Rufilla had many slave-girls.*

Further examples:

  a Bregāns magnum taurum dūcēbat.
  b coquus amīcīs parvam cēnam parāvit.
  c multī Britannī erant servī.
  d agricola parvīs puerīs equum ostendit.

in tablīnō

postrīdiē Salvius et Philus in tablīnō sunt. intrat Rūfilla.

Rūfilla:	mī Salvī!	**mī Salvī!** *my dear Salvius!*
Salvius:	occupātus sum! necesse est mihi hās epistulās dictāre. ego rem celeriter cōnficere volō. ubi est sella mea? 5	
	(Salvius sellam frūstrā quaerit.)	
	heus! ubi est ista sella?	**heus!** *hey!*
Rūfilla:	mī cārissime! aliquid tibi dīcere volō.	**cārissime** *dearest*
Salvius:	tē nunc audīre nōn possum. epistulās dictāre volō. ecce! Philus parātus adest. stilī et cērae adsunt – *10* heus! ubi est armārium meum? quis cēpit?	**aliquid** *something*
Rūfilla:	Salvī! audī!	
	(tandem Salvius uxōrī cēdit et Philum dīmittit.)	**cēdit: cēdere** *give in, give way*
Salvius:	ēheu! abī, Phile! nōn commodum est mihi epistulās dictāre. *15*	
Rūfilla:	bene! nunc aliquid tibi dīcere possum. ubi in urbe Londiniō nūper eram, familiārem convēnī.	**bene!** *good!* **nūper** *recently*
Salvius:	tot familiārēs habēs! eōs numerāre nōn possum.	**convēnī: convenīre** *meet*
Rūfilla:	sed hic familiāris est Quīntus Caecilius Iūcundus. ubi mōns Vesuvius urbem Pompēiōs dēlēvit, *20* Quīntus ex urbe effūgit. quam cōmis est! quam urbānus!	**tot** *so many* **cōmis** *courteous, friendly* **urbānus** *smart, fashionable*
Salvius:	hercle! ego Pompēiānīs nōn crēdō. paucī probī sunt, cēterī mendācēs. ubi in Campāniā mīlitābam, multōs Pompēiānōs cognōscēbam. mercātōrēs Pompēiānī *25* nōs mīlitēs semper dēcipiēbant.	**paucī** *a few* **mīlitābam: mīlitāre** *be a soldier* **cognōscēbam: cognōscere** *get to know*
Rūfilla:	stultissimus es! familiāris meus nōn est mercātor. Quīntus vir nōbilis est. eum ad vīllam nostram invītāvī.	**mīlitēs: mīles** *soldier*
Salvius:	quid dīxistī? Pompēiānum invītāvistī? ad vīllam nostram? *30*	
Rūfilla:	decōrum est mihi familiārem meum hūc invītāre. ancillae familiārī meō cubiculum parāvērunt. ancillae, quod cubiculum inēlegāns erat, sellam armāriumque tuum in eō posuērunt.	**in eō** *in it*
Salvius:	īnsāna es, uxor! Pompēiānī mendāciōrēs sunt quam *35* Britannī. num tū sellam et armārium ē tablīnō extrāxistī?	**num tū… extrāxistī?** *surely you did not take?*
Rūfilla:	et candēlābrum.	**prō dī immortālēs!** *heavens above!*
Salvius:	prō dī immortālēs! ō candēlābrum meum! ō mē miserum! *40*	**ō mē miserum!** *oh wretched me! oh dear!*

About the language 2: more about adjectives

1   In the first language note in this Stage you met sentences like this:

        cīvis servum **bonum** salūtāvit.   *The citizen greeted the good slave.*

    The adjective **bonum** agrees with the noun **servum** in case
(accusative) and number (singular). The endings of both words
look the same.

2   Now study this sentence:

        cīvis servum **trīstem** salūtāvit.   *The citizen greeted the sad slave.*

    The adjective **trīstem** agrees with the noun **servum** in case
(accusative) and number (singular) as in the previous example.
The endings, however, do not look the same. This is because they
belong to different declensions, and have different ways of
forming their cases. **trīstis** belongs to the third declension and
servus belongs to the second declension.

3   Translate the following examples:

    a   Quīntus fābulam mīrābilem nārrāvit.
    b   in vīllā habitābat senex stultus.
    c   gladiātor bēstiās ferōcēs agitābat.
    d   dominus amīcō fidēlī dēnāriōs trādidit.
    e   multī mercātōrēs vīnum bibēbant.
    f   agricola omnibus puerīs pecūniam dedit.

    Write down the Latin noun and adjective pair in each sentence and
state whether the pair is nominative, accusative or dative, singular
or plural.

*A wax tablet with a
government stamp on the
back. Salvius, as a Roman
administrator, may have used
official tablets like this one.*

Quīntus advenit

When you have read this story, answer the questions below.

Quīntus ad vīllam advēnit. Salvius ē vīllā contendit et eum
salūtāvit.

'mī Quīnte!' inquit. 'exspectātissimus es! cubiculum optimum
tibi parāvimus.'

Salvius Quīntum in tablīnum dūxit, ubi Rūfilla sedēbat.   5
Rūfilla, postquam familiārem suum salūtāvit, suāviter rīsit.

• 'cēnam modicam tibi parāvī', inquit. 'tibi ostreās parāvī et
garum Pompēiānum. post cēnam cubiculum tibi ostendere
volō.'

Salvius, postquam Quīntus cēnam cōnsūmpsit, dē urbe   10
Pompēiīs quaerēbat.

'ubi in Campāniā mīlitābam, saepe urbem Pompēiōs
vīsitābam. nōnne illa clādēs terribilis erat?'

Rūfilla interpellāvit,

'cūr Quīntum nostrum vexās? nōn decōrum est. difficile est   15
Quīntō tantam clādem commemorāre.'

Rūfilla ad Quīntum sē convertit.

'fortasse, mī Quīnte, fessus es. cubiculum tibi parāvī.
cubiculum nōn est ōrnātum. in eō sunt armārium modicum et
candēlābrum parvum.'   20

Salvius īrātus nihil dīxit.

Quīntus, postquam cubiculum vīdit, exclāmāvit,

'quam ēlegāns est cubiculum! ego nihil ēlegantius vīdī.'

'cōnsentiō', inquit Salvius. 'cubiculum tuum ēlegantius est
quam tablīnum meum.'   25

exspectātissimus: exspectātus
welcome

modicam *ordinary, little*
ostreās: ostrea *oyster*
garum *sauce*

clādēs *disaster*
terribilis *terrible*
interpellāvit: interpellāre
interrupt
tantam *so great, such a great*
commemorāre *talk about*
sē convertit: sē convertere
turn
ōrnātum: ōrnātus
*elaborately furnished,
decorated*
ēlegantius *more tasteful*

Questions

		Marks
1	Find four examples in this story where Salvius and Rufilla are not telling the truth. In each case, explain why their words are untrue.	4 + 4
2	Why do you think Quintus says so little in this story? Think of two reasons.	2
		TOTAL 10

tripodes argenteī

Quīntus in cubiculō sedet. Anti-Loquāx celeriter intrat.

Anti-Loquāx:	salvē! necesse est dominō meō ad aulam īre. rēx Cogidubnus omnēs nōbilēs ad sacrificium invītāvit.
Quīntus:	rēgem hodiē vīsitāmus?
Anti-Loquāx:	ita vērō. quotannīs rēx sacrificium facit, quod imperātōrem Claudium honōrāre vult.
Quīntus:	cūr Claudium honōrāre vult?
Anti-Loquāx:	decōrum est Cogidubnō Claudium honōrāre. nam Claudius erat imperātor quī Cogidubnum rēgem fēcit.
Quīntus:	nunc rem intellegō. necesse est mihi dōnum rēgī ferre. in arcā meā sunt duo tripodes argenteī. illī tripodes sunt dōnum optimum.
	(Anti-Loquāx ē cubiculō exit et Salviō dē tripodibus argenteīs nārrat. Salvius statim ad cellārium contendit.)
Salvius:	necesse est mihi rēgem Cogidubnum vīsitāre. dōnum eī ferre volō.
cellārius:	nōn difficile est nōbīs dōnum invenīre, domine. ecce! urna aēnea. antīquissima est. placetne tibi?
Salvius:	mihi nōn placet. dōnum aēneum Cogidubnō ferre nōlō.

tripodes *tripods*
argenteī: argenteus
 made of silver

aulam: aula *palace*

5

quotannīs *every year*
imperātōrem: imperātor
 emperor
honōrāre *honour*

10

arcā: arca *strong-box, chest*

15

cellārium: cellārius *steward*

20

urna *jar, jug*

	(cellārius Salviō amphoram dēmōnstrat.)	**amphoram: amphora** *wine-jar*
		dēmōnstrat: dēmōnstrāre
cellārius:	nōnne vīnum est dōnum optimum, domine? 25	*point out, show*
Salvius:	minimē! Cogidubnus multās amphorās habet,	
	multumque vīnum. rēx vīnum ex Ītaliā cotīdiē	
	importat.	**importat: importāre** *import*
	(subitō Salvius statuam parvam cōnspicit.)	
	euge! hanc statuam rēgī ferre possum. aurāta est 30	**aurāta** *gilded, gold-plated*
	statua. Quīntus rēgī dōnum argenteum ferre vult;	
	ego tamen aurātum dōnum ferre possum!	
cellārius:	domine! nōn dēbēs.	**nōn dēbēs**
Salvius:	cūr nōn dēbeō?	*you shouldn't, you mustn't*
cellārius:	Cogidubnus ipse tibi illam statuam dedit! 35	
Salvius:	hercle! necesse est mihi istam urnam ad aulam	
	ferre.	

The British aristocracy loved Roman silver. This elegant wine cup was made about the time of our story. It is one of several found buried in Norfolk.

Practising the language

1   Complete each sentence with the right form of the adjective. Then translate the sentence.

a	servī canem . . . . retrāxērunt.	(ferōx, ferōcem)
b	mercātor . . . . pecūniam āmīsit.	(stultus, stultum)
c	ego . . . . iuvenēs in forō vīdī.	(multī, multōs)
d	ōrnātrīx . . . . coquō ōsculum dedit.	(laeta, laetam)
e	amīcī . . . . lībertum servāvērunt.	(fortēs, fortibus)
f	māter . . . . puerīs cibum parāvit.	(parvī, parvōs, parvīs)
g	Bregāns amphoram . . . . portāre nōlēbat.	(gravis, gravem, gravī)
h	domina ancillae . . . . stolam ēmit.	(fidēlis, fidēlem, fidēlī)

2   Complete each sentence with the right form of the imperfect tense
    from the list below and then translate. You will have to use one
    word more than once.

eram	erāmus
erās	erātis
erat	erant

a   vīlicus . . . . anxius; nam Salvius . . . . īrātus.
b   vōs gladiōs habēbātis quod vōs . . . . custōdēs.
c   servī . . . . in āreā, ubi Salvium exspectābant.
d   tū . . . . dominus; decōrum . . . . tibi celeriter prōcēdere.
e   nōs nōn . . . . ignāvī; in fundō dīligenter labōrābāmus.
f   ego in cubiculō iacēbam quod aeger . . . .

The Romans in Britain

The British tribes

Before the Roman invasion, the Britons lived in tribes, usually ruled by a king or queen. A chieftain was a wealthy landowner who controlled a very small area and owed his loyalty to a king or queen. Most chieftains maintained a band of warriors who practised their fighting skills by hunting wild animals and raiding settlements belonging to other tribes. Many families owned slaves.

Religion was in the hands of the Druids. These powerful priests, who acted as judges in disputes, worshipped the gods in sacred woodlands with ceremonies that sometimes included human sacrifice. They encouraged fierce British resistance to the Roman invasion.

The conquest

The first Roman general to lead his soldiers into Britain was Julius Caesar, in 55 BC. Caesar wrote an account of his visit to Britain, in which he described the inhabitants as fierce warriors, living on good agricultural or pasture land, in a country rich in timber and minerals. Their skills included not only farming, but also making pottery and working with iron and bronze.

Caesar wanted to find out whether the rewards to be gained by occupying Britain were worth the trouble of launching a major military campaign. But after another short visit in 54 BC, he did not explore any further. His attention was diverted by wars elsewhere, first against the Gauls and then against his own Roman government. Ten years later, he was assassinated.

Caesar's great-nephew Augustus became the first Roman emperor. He and his immediate successors did not consider Britain to be worth the trouble of conquering. But in AD 43 the Emperor Claudius decided to invade. Perhaps he had received fresh information about British wealth; more probably he needed some military success for his own prestige. Claudius did not lead the invasion force himself, but he followed it. He spent sixteen days in Britain, watching his army's assault on Colchester (Camulodunum) and giving official approval to the actions of his commander Aulus Plautius.

Eleven British kings surrendered after this campaign, and Britain was declared a Roman province, with Aulus Plautius as its first governor. This meant that the Romans were taking over the country as part of their empire. From then on, Roman officials would enforce Roman law and collect Roman taxes. Romans would be able to buy land in Britain and use it for agriculture or mining. And the Roman army would be present to keep the peace in the province, firmly and sometimes brutally.

Skull of a pre-conquest Briton, who was buried with a crown on his head.

The Romans who conquered: Julius Caesar (above) *and the Emperor Claudius* (below).

Some British rulers, like King Cogidubnus in the south, chose to co-operate with the invaders and became allies and dependants of Rome. Others, such as Caratacus in Wales, and Queen Boudica in East Anglia, resisted the Romans bitterly but unsuccessfully. The Romans gradually moved further north, occupying the Midlands and Wales, then the northern kingdom of Brigantia and finally part of Scotland.

The stories in Stages 13 and 14 are set in the time of Britain's most famous governor, Gnaeus Julius Agricola. Agricola stayed in the province for seven years (AD 78–85). He led his army into the Scottish highlands where he built a number of forts, some of which have only recently been discovered. He effectively put an end to Scottish resistance in AD 84 by defeating their army at the battle of Mons Graupius near Aberdeen.

Romanisation and trade

Agricola's mission in Britain was not just military victory. His son-in-law, the historian Tacitus, says: 'He wanted to accustom the Britons to a life of peace by providing them with the comforts of civilisation. He gave personal encouragement and official aid to the building of temples, forums and houses… He educated the sons of the chiefs… so that instead of hating the Latin language, they were eager to speak it well.'

In Stage 13 we saw how some British farmers began to build villas in the Roman style. Towns, too, were built or rebuilt on the Roman grid system, with forums, temples and other public buildings similar to those in Roman Gaul. Gradually, a network

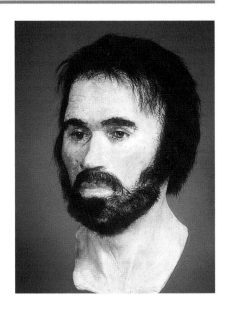

This is an artist's reconstruction of the head of a man whose body was found preserved in a peat bog. The Britons may have sacrificed him to their gods, perhaps in an attempt to keep the Romans away.

Aulus Plautius' men dug these ditches to defend their camp at Rutupiae (Richborough). The fortress walls were added later, in the third century AD.

Claudius built a triumphal arch at Rome to celebrate the capture of Britain. Part of the inscription survives (right). Claudius also pictured the arch on his coins.

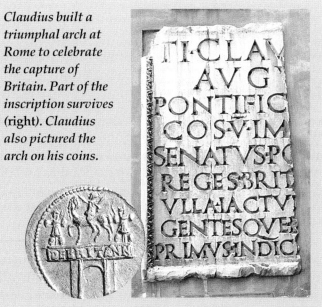

of new roads spread across the province. The roads were originally built for the use of Roman soldiers; but before long they were being extensively used by merchants as well. Trade between Britain and the continent increased rapidly.

Some Britons became very wealthy from trade and welcomed the Romans enthusiastically; many of the leading families responded to Agricola's encouragement to adopt a Roman lifestyle. On the other hand, some Britons suffered severely from the arrival of the Romans, whilst others were hardly affected at all. Many no doubt had mixed feelings about becoming part of the Roman empire. It gave them a share in Roman prosperity and the Roman way of life; but it also meant Roman taxes and a Roman governor backed by Roman troops. However, whether the Britons liked it or not, the Romans were to remain in their country for nearly four hundred years.

Watling Street, passing through Northamptonshire.

The Romans set up cities in Britain, with forums and temples. This is a model of the temple of the deified Emperor Claudius at Colchester.

Boudica

Boudica was the wife of King Prasutagus, king of the Iceni, a tribe who lived in East Anglia. On the death of Prasutagus all his lands and property were confiscated by the Romans, Boudica was flogged and her daughters raped. Boudica and the Iceni would not let these unprovoked insults go unavenged and, joining with other discontented tribes, they raised a rebellion (AD 60).

At first the rebels were very successful. They met with no effective opposition, since the Roman governor, Suetonius Paulinus, was far away in Anglesey (Mona) fighting the Druids and their supporters. Boudica's forces looted and destroyed the Roman town of Colchester, killing all the inhabitants. London

Boudica leading her warriors, according to the sculpture on the Thames Embankment in London.

(Londinium) and St Albans (Verulamium) suffered the same fate. Eventually Suetonius Paulinus confronted Boudica and her forces with his legions. Although the Roman troops were heavily outnumbered, their superior training and tactics won them a decisive victory. Rather than face capture, Boudica committed suicide by taking poison.

In Roman eyes Boudica was a remarkable and fearsome figure, not only because she brought them to the brink of disaster, but also because she was a woman who wielded real power. In this she was not alone among British women. From the little we know of their lives, some from the wealthier families had equal rights with men. They could own property in their own right within marriage, divorce their husbands and, after death, be buried with precious possessions, with the same funeral rites as their menfolk. By contrast, even high-born Roman women like Rufilla, although they had an important role to play in running their households, were legally under the control of a male relative. It is not surprising therefore that Boudica was regarded by the Romans as an unnatural, dangerous but fascinating woman.

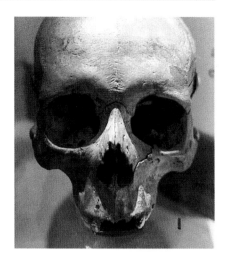

Finds from the towns she captured illustrate the havoc Boudica caused. This skull, found in London, may have belonged to a man killed by Boudica's army.

At Colchester, the Iceni massacred some of the inhabitants who had taken refuge in the temple of Claudius. They then burned the city. Archaeologists have found a thick layer of burned debris, including the broken stock of a pottery shop (above) and some charred dates (above right) – both imported goods. The bronze head of Claudius (right) was probably wrenched from one of his statues in the city and thrown into a river.

Britain in the first century AD

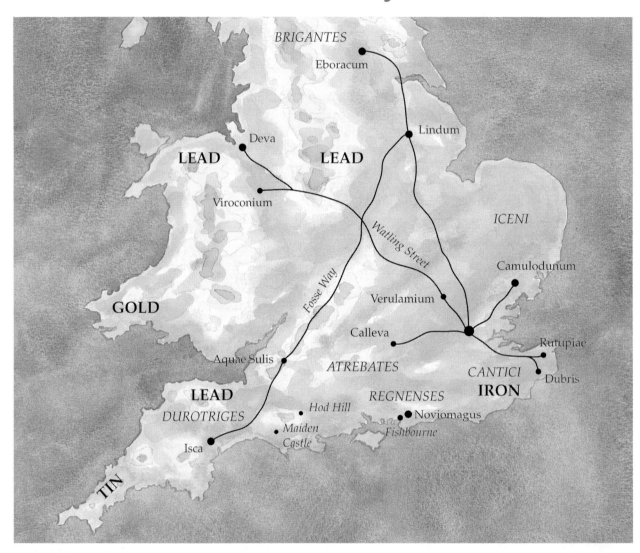

BRIGANTES

Eboracum

Deva

LEAD   **LEAD**

Viroconium

Lindum

Watling Street

Fosse Way

ICENI

Camulodunum

Verulamium

Calleva

Rutupiae

GOLD

Aquae Sulis

ATREBATES

CANTICI

IRON

Dubris

LEAD

REGNENSES

DUROTRIGES

Hod Hill

Noviomagus

Maiden Castle

Fishbourne

Isca

TIN

Imports and exports

A lead miner.

Among the items exported from Britain in Roman times were grain, hunting dogs and metals: iron, gold, tin and lead. In return, Britain imported wine, oil and other goods from Rome and the rest of the empire.

A wealthy Briton who died shortly before the Roman conquest was already importing wine. He had jars of it (amphorae) buried with him.

Important events and dates

Emperor	Year	Event
	BC	
	55–54	Julius Caesar's expeditions to Britain.
	44	*Caesar assassinated.*
Augustus	27	*The first emperor.*
	AD	
Tiberius	14	
Gaius (Caligula)	37	
Claudius	41	

	43	Invasion of Britain under Aulus Plautius. Claudius enters Colchester in triumph. Vespasian's expedition against the Durotriges. Britain becomes a Roman province.
	51	Defeat of Caratacus in Wales.
Nero	54	
	60/61	Revolt of Boudica in East Anglia.
Vespasian	69	*Civil War in Italy.*
	75	The building of Fishbourne palace begins.
	78	Agricola comes to Britain as Governor.
Titus	79	*Eruption of Vesuvius.*
	80	Agricola's Scottish campaigns begin.
Domitian	81	Salvius is sent to Britain.
	84	Battle of Mons Graupius.
Honorius	410	Romans cease to defend Britain.

Vocabulary checklist 14

aliquid	something	fidēlis	faithful, loyal
apud	among, at the house of	ipse, ipsa	himself, herself
attonitus	astonished	iste	that
aula	palace	marītus	husband
cotīdiē	every day	necesse	necessary
decōrus	right, proper	num?	surely… not?
dēleō, dēlēre, dēlēvī	destroy	quam	how
deus	god	quamquam	although
difficilis	difficult	-que	and
dīligenter	carefully	rēx	king
domina	mistress	ubi	when
dōnum	present, gift		

Detail of a Roman cavalryman's gravestone. A conquered Briton cowers beneath the horse's hooves.

REX COGIDUBNUS

STAGE 15

1 multī Britannī ad aulam vēnērunt.
senex, quī scēptrum tenēbat, erat rēx
Cogidubnus.

2 fēmina prope Cogidubnum sedēbat.
fēmina, quae diadēma gerēbat, erat
rēgīna.

3 multī Rōmānī Cogidubnō rēs pretiōsās
dabant. dōnum, quod rēgem valdē
dēlectāvit, erat equus.

4 duae ancillae ad rēgem vēnērunt.
vīnum, quod ancillae ferēbant, erat in
paterā aureā. rēx vīnum lībāvit.

5 servus agnum ad āram dūxit. agnus,
quem servus dūcēbat, erat victima.

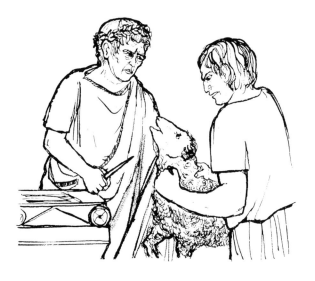

6 sacerdōs victimam īnspexit. victima,
quam servus tenēbat, bālāvit. sacerdōs
victimam interfēcit.

ad aulam

agmen longissimum ad aulam prōcēdēbat. in prīmā parte ībant decem
servī. hī servī, quī virgās longās tenēbant, erant praecursōrēs. in mediō
agmine Salvius et Quīntus equitābant. post eōs ambulābant trēs
ancillae, quae urnam et tripodas portābant. aliae ancillae flōrēs
ferēbant. postrēmō prōcēdēbant vīgintī servī. agmen, quod tōtam viam 5
complēbat, erat splendidum.

    multī quoque Britannī cum uxōribus ad aulam ībant. magna turba
erat in viā. tum Vārica, quī cum praecursōribus equitābat, ad Salvium
rediit.

Vārica:	domine, difficile est nōbīs prōcēdere, quod hī *10*
	Britannī viam complent. ē viā exīre nōlunt. quid
	facere dēbeō?
Salvius:	*(īrātus)* necesse est praecursōribus Britannōs ē viā
	ēmovēre. nōn decōrum est Britannīs cīvēs Rōmānōs
	impedīre. ego quam celerrimē īre volō, quod rēx nōs *15*
	exspectat.

    (Vārica, quī dominum īrātum timēbat, ad praecursōrēs
rediit.)

Vārica: asinī estis! virgās habētis. ēmovēte Britannōs!

tum praecursōrēs statim virgās vibrābant. multī Britannī in fossās   *20*
dēsiluērunt, quod virgās timēbant. duo iuvenēs tamen impavidī in viā
cōnsistēbant. prope iuvenēs erat plaustrum, quod tōtam viam
claudēbat.

agmen *procession*
in prīmā parte *in the forefront*
virgās: virga *rod, stick*
praecursōrēs: praecursor
   forerunner (sent ahead of a
   procession to clear the way)
equitābant: equitāre *ride*
flōrēs: flōs *flower*

facere dēbeō *ought to do*

ēmovēre *move, clear away*
impedīre *delay, hinder*

fossās: fossa *ditch*
dēsiluērunt: dēsilīre *jump*
   down
impavidī: impavidus *fearless*
cōnsistēbant: cōnsistere
   stand one's ground, stand firm
plaustrum *wagon, cart*
claudēbat: claudere *block*

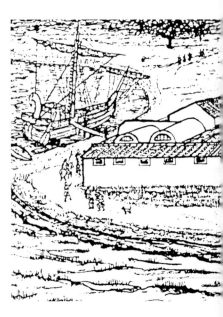

aula

Vārica:	cūr viam clauditis? necesse est dominō meō ad aulam īre.	25
iuvenis prīmus:	nōs quoque ad aulam contendimus. rēgem vīsitāre volumus. sed plaustrum movēre nōn possumus, quod plaustrum rotam frāctam habet.	**movēre** *move* **rotam: rota** *wheel*
iuvenis secundus:	amīcus noster, quem nōs exspectāmus, aliam rotam quaerit. amīcum exspectāre dēbēmus.	30

(Vārica anxius ad Salvium iterum rediit.)

Vārica:	plaustrum, quod vidēs, domine, rotam frāctam habet. difficile est nōbīs prōcēdere, quod hoc plaustrum tōtam viam claudit.	35
Salvius:	*(īrātior quam anteā)* num surdus es? caudex! nōn commodum est mihi in hōc locō manēre. quam celerrimē prōcēdere volō.	**anteā** *before* **surdus** *deaf*

(Vārica ad praecursōrēs iterum rediit.)

Vārica:	caudicēs! ēmovēte hoc plaustrum! dēicite in fossam!	40	**dēicite!** *throw!*

praecursōrēs, postquam Vāricam audīvērunt, plaustrum in fossam dēiēcērunt. iuvenēs, quī erant attonitī, vehementer resistēbant et cum praecursōribus pugnābant. tum praecursōrēs iuvenēs quoque in fossam dēiēcērunt. Salvius, quī rem spectābat, per viam prōcessit.

resistēbant: resistere *resist*

45

Salvius:	*(cachinnāns)* Britannī sunt molestissimī. semper nōs Rōmānōs vexant.	**cachinnāns** *laughing, cackling* **molestissimī: molestus** *troublesome*

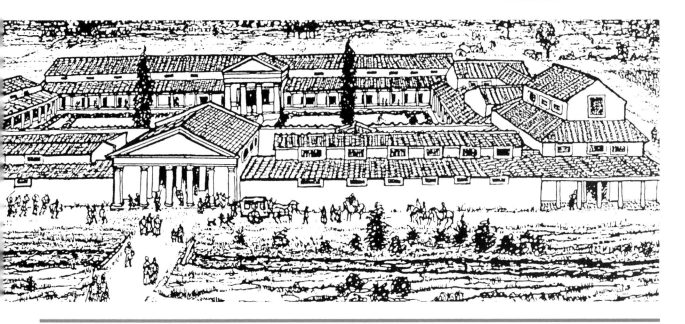

caerimōnia

When you have read this story, answer the questions on page 49.

servus Salvium et Quīntum ad ātrium dūxit. illī, postquam
ātrium intrāvērunt, magnam turbam vīdērunt. multī prīncipēs
Britannicī multaeque fēminae in ātriō erant. sermōnēs inter sē
habēbant. aderant quoque multī Rōmānī, quī prope prīncipēs
sedēbant. haec multitūdō, quae ātrium complēbat, magnum   5
clāmōrem faciēbat.

in mediō ātriō Quīntus et Salvius lectum vīdērunt. in lectō erat
effigiēs cērāta. Quīntus effigiem agnōvit.

'bona est effigiēs!' inquit. 'imperātor Claudius est!'

'ita vērō', respondit Salvius. 'rēx Cogidubnus Claudium   10
quotannīs honōrat. fabrī ex Italiā quotannīs veniunt. fabrī, quī
perītissimī sunt, effigiem faciunt.'

subitō turba, quae prope iānuam stābat, ad terram prōcubuit.
prīncipēs Britannicī, quī in mediō ātriō sedēbant, celeriter
surrēxērunt. etiam Rōmānī tacēbant.   15

'rēx adest', susurrāvit Salvius.

per iānuam intrāvit senex. parvus puer senem dūcēbat, quod
claudicābat. rēx et puer lentē per turbam prōcēdēbant. rēx,
postquam ad effigiem advēnit, vīnum lībāvit. tum sacerdōtēs,
quī prope effigiem stābant, victimās ad rēgem dūxērunt.   20
Cogidubnus victimās dīligenter īnspexit. victima, quam rēx
ēlēgit, erat agnus niveus. rēx eum sacrificāvit.

'decōrum est nōbīs Claudium honōrāre', inquit.

sacerdōtēs quoque victimās cēterās sacrificāvērunt. tum
decem prīncipēs Britannicī lectum in umerōs sustulērunt.   25
effigiem ex ātriō portāvērunt. post prīncipēs vēnērunt
sacerdōtēs, quī sollemniter cantābant.

in āreā erat rogus. prīncipēs, quī effigiem portābant, ad rogum
cum magnā dignitāte prōcessērunt. effigiem in rogum
posuērunt. servus rēgī facem trādidit. tum rēx facem in rogum   30
posuit. mox flammae rogum cōnsūmēbant. flammae, quae
effigiem iam tangēbant, cēram liquābant. omnēs effigiem intentē
spectābant. subitō aquila ex effigiē ēvolāvit. omnēs spectātōrēs
plausērunt.

'ecce!' inquit rēx. 'deī Claudium arcessunt. animus ad deōs   35
ascendit.'

caerimōnia *ceremony*

ātrium *hall*
illī *they*
prīncipēs: prīnceps *chief,
    chieftain*
Britannicī: Britannicus *British*
sermōnēs: sermō *conversation*
inter sē *among themselves, with
    each other*
multitūdō *crowd*
effigiēs cērāta *wax image*
bona *good*
fabrī: faber *craftsman*
prōcubuit: prōcumbere *fall*
claudicābat: claudicāre
    be lame, limp
vīnum lībāvit
    poured wine as an offering
sacerdōtēs: sacerdōs *priest*
victimās: victima *victim*
agnus *lamb*
niveus *snow-white*
sacrificāvit: sacrificāre
    sacrifice
umerōs: umerus *shoulder*
sustulērunt: tollere *raise, lift up*
sollemniter cantābant
    were chanting solemnly
rogus *pyre*
cum magnā dignitāte
    with great dignity
facem: fax *torch*
tangēbant: tangere *touch*
liquābant: liquāre *melt*
aquila *eagle*
ēvolāvit: ēvolāre *fly out*
arcessunt: arcessere
    summon, send for
animus *soul, spirit*
ascendit: ascendere *climb, rise*

Questions

		Marks
1	Where was the crowd gathered for the ceremony? Which three groups of people did Salvius and Quintus see there (lines 2–5)?	2
2	**haec multitūdō** (line 5). Suggest two English adjectives which you think best describe the crowd in this sentence.	2
3	Where was the wax image? Whom did it represent (lines 7–9)?	1 + 1
4	**bona est effigiēs**. How did Salvius explain the good quality of the image (lines 11–12)?	2
5	In lines 13–15, how did the different sections of the crowd behave?	2 + 1 + 1
6	Why was the king accompanied by a boy (lines 17–18)?	1
7	In lines 18–22 what two offerings did the king make? How did the priests assist the king in this ceremony?	2 + 1
8	After the priests sacrificed their victims, what did the British chieftains do (lines 25–6)?	2
9	Where was the image placed (lines 28–30)?	1
10	**servus rēgī facem trādidit**. What did the king do with the torch? What then happened to the image (lines 30–2)?	2
11	In lines 33–4, why did the spectators applaud?	1
12	What two things did the king say about Claudius (lines 35–6)? What did the **aquila** represent?	2 + 1

TOTAL **25**

mox flammae rogum cōnsūmēbant.

About the language 1: relative clauses

1   Study the following pair of sentences:

>   ancilla urnam portābat.
>   *The slave-girl was carrying the jug.*

>   ancilla, **quae post Salvium ambulābat**, urnam portābat.
>   *The slave-girl, **who was walking behind Salvius**, was carrying the jug.*

The group of words in **bold type** is known as a relative clause.

2   A relative clause is used to describe a noun. For example:

>   vīlicus, **quī cum praecursōribus equitābat**, ad Salvium rediit.
>   *The farm manager, **who was riding with the forerunners**, returned to Salvius.*

>   prope iuvenēs erat plaustrum, **quod tōtam viam claudēbat**.
>   *Near the young men was a wagon, **which was blocking the whole road**.*

In the first example, the relative clause describes the farm manager; in the second, the relative clause describes the wagon.

3   Translate the following examples:

a   rēx, quī scēptrum tenēbat, in ātriō sedēbat.
b   vīnum, quod Salvius bibēbat, erat optimum.
c   ancillae, quae dominum timēbant, ē vīllā festīnāvērunt.
d   canis, quem Bregāns dūcēbat, ferōcissimus erat.
e   in viā erant multī Britannī, quī Rōmānōs impediēbant.
f   cēna, quam Volūbilis parābat, erat splendida.

For each example, write down the Latin relative clause and the Latin noun it describes.

lūdī fūnebrēs

I

post caerimōniam rēx Cogidubnus pompam ad lītus dūxit. ibi Britannī lūdōs fūnebrēs celebrāvērunt. aderant Rēgnēnsēs, Canticī et aliae gentēs Britannicae.

competītōrēs diū inter sē certābant. Canticī laetissimī erant, quod semper vincēbant. āthlēta Canticus, quī celerrimē cucurrit, 5
cēterōs facile superāvit. alter āthlēta Canticus, quī perītissimus erat, discum longius quam cēterī ēmīsit.

postrēmō Cogidubnus certāmen nāvāle inter Canticōs et Rēgnēnsēs nūntiāvit. Belimicus nāvī Canticae praeerat; prīnceps Canticus erat, homō superbus et īnsolēns. Dumnorix, quī alterī 10
nāvī praeerat, prīnceps Rēgnēnsis erat, vir fortis et probus. nautae, postquam nāvēs parāvērunt, signum intentē exspectābant. subitō tuba sonuit. nāvēs statim per undās ruērunt. spectātōrēs, quī in lītore stābant, magnōs clāmōrēs sustulērunt. 15

pompam: pompa *procession*
ad lītus *to the sea-shore*
gentēs: gēns *tribe*
competītōrēs: competītor
  competitor
certābant: certāre *compete*
vincēbant: vincere
  be victorious, win
longius *further*
certāmen nāvāle *boat-race*
inter Canticōs et Rēgnēnsēs
  between the Cantici and the
  Regnenses
superbus *arrogant, proud*
undās: unda *wave*
in lītore *on the shore*

II

procul in marī erat saxum ingēns. hoc saxum erat mēta. nāvēs ad
mētam ruēbant. nāvis Rēgnēnsis, quam Dumnorix dīrigēbat,
iam prior erat. Dumnorix, ubi saxō appropinquāvit, nāvem
subitō ad dextram vertit.

'ecce!' inquit Dumnorix. 'perīculōsum est nōbīs prope saxum   5
nāvigāre, quod scopulus sub undīs latet. necesse est nōbīs
scopulum vītāre.'

Belimicus tamen, quī scopulum ignōrābat, cursum rēctum
tenēbat.

'amīcī', clāmāvit, 'nōs vincere possumus, quod Dumnorix ad   10
dextram abiit. hī Rēgnēnsēs sunt timidī; facile est nōbīs vincere,
quod nōs sumus fortiōrēs.'

nautae Canticī Belimicō crēdēbant. mox nāvem Rēgnēnsem
superāvērunt et priōrēs mētae appropinquāvērunt. Belimicus,
quī scopulum nōn vīdit, Dumnorigem dērīdēbat. subitō nāvis   15
Cantica in scopulum incurrit. nautae perterritī clāmāvērunt;
aqua nāvem complēbat. Belimicus et Canticī nihil facere
poterant; nāvis mox summersa erat.

intereā Dumnorix, quī cum summā cūrā nāvigābat, circum
mētam nāvem dīrēxit. nāvis ad lītus incolumis pervēnit. multī   20
spectātōrēs Dumnorigem laudāvērunt. Rēgnēnsēs laetī, Canticī
miserī erant. tum omnēs ad mare oculōs vertēbant. difficile erat
eīs nautās vidēre, quod in undīs natābant. omnēs tamen
Belimicum vidēre poterant, quod in summō saxō sedēbat.
madidus ad saxum haerēbat et auxilium postulābat.   25

About the language 2: imperfect tense of possum, etc

1   In Stage 13, you met the present tense of **possum**, 'I am able':

> Loquāx currere potest.   ego labōrāre nōn possum.
> *Loquax is able to run.*   *I am not able to work.*

2   You have also met **possum** in the imperfect tense:

> Loquāx currere poterat.   ego labōrāre nōn poteram.
> *Loquax was able to run.*   *I wasn't able to work.*
> or *Loquax could run.*   or *I couldn't work.*

3   The complete imperfect tense of **possum** is:

(ego)	poteram	*I was able* or *I could*
(tū)	poterās	*you (singular) were able*
	poterat	*he was able*
(nōs)	poterāmus	*we were able*
(vōs)	poterātis	*you (plural) were able*
	poterant	*they were able*

4   Further examples:

a   servī sōlem vidēre nōn poterant.
b   Bregāns amphoram portāre nōn poterat.
c   nōs labōrāre poterāmus.
d   in urbe manēre nōn poterās.

5   The imperfect tenses of **volō** and **nōlō** are formed in the same way
as the imperfect of **trahō**: **volēbam**, 'I was willing', 'I wanted';
nōlēbam, 'I was unwilling', 'I did not want'.

6   Translate the following examples:

a   Rūfilla vīllam prope urbem habēre volēbat.
b   nōs redīre nōlēbāmus.
c   servum interficere nōlēbant.
d   cūr festīnāre volēbās?

Practising the language

1   Complete each sentence with the right form of the noun and then translate.

   a   parvus puer . . . . ad effigiem dūxit. (Cogidubnum, Cogidubnō)
   b   ubi sacerdōtēs erant parātī, servī vīnum . . . . dedērunt. (rēgem, rēgī)
   c   Cogidubnus, quī prope effigiem stābat, ... ēlēgit. (victimam, victimae)
   d   Dumnorix nāvem . . . . ostendit. (amīcōs, amīcīs)
   e   facile erat . . . . Belimicum vidēre, quod ad saxum haerēbat.
        (spectātōrēs, spectātōribus)
   f   postquam Dumnorix Belimicum superāvit, rēx . . . . ad aulam invītāvit.
        (nautās, nautīs)

2   Translate the following sentences:

   a   difficile est Cogidubnō festīnāre, quod senex est.
   b   spectāculum vidēre nōlumus.
   c   necesse est nōbīs fugere.
   d   pecūniam reddere dēbēs.
   e   Salvius est dominus; decōrum est Salviō servōs pūnīre.
   f   commodum est tibi in aulā manēre.
   g   victimam sacrificāre vīs?
   h   pugnāre nōn dēbēmus!

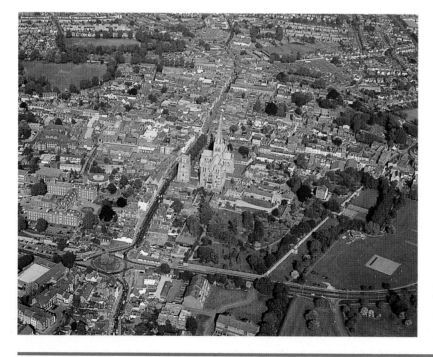

Aerial view of Chichester. The town walls and the intersecting main streets were laid out in Roman times.

Cogidubnus, king of the Regnenses

```
NEPTVNO·ET·MINERVAE
      TEMPLVM
PRO·SALVTE·DOMVS·DIVINAE
EX·AVCTORITATE·TI·C·LAVD·
COGIDVBNI·REG·MAGNI·BRIT·
COLEGIVM·FABROR·ET·QVI·IN·EO·
SVNT·D·S·D·DONANTE·AREAM·
   ENTE·PVDENTINI·FIL·
```

A drawing of what remains of the inscription. Some missing letters have been put in according to what is most likely to have been there. The photograph on page 43 shows part of the original stone. You can read the end of Cogidubnus' name. Notice there the neat carving of the well-proportioned letters.

To Neptune and Minerva, for the welfare of the Divine House, by the authority of Tiberius Claudius Cogidubnus, great king of the Britons, the Guild of Smiths and those in it gave this temple at their own expense. …ens, son of Pudentinus, presented the forecourt.

A slab of stone inscribed with these Latin words was discovered near the Sussex coast in Chichester in 1723. When found, the slab was broken, but as soon as the pieces had been fitted together it was clear that this was the dedication stone of a temple built at the request of Cogidubnus in honour of Neptune, god of the sea, and Minerva, goddess of wisdom and craftsmanship. The elegant lettering, carved in the style of the first century AD, suggested the work of Roman craftsmen. Roman dedication stones are rather like the foundation stones which are laid nowadays when an important public building, such as a church, library or school, is being erected. They state the name of the person or group of people who gave the site and paid for the building. This particular building was paid for by the local **collēgium** or guild of smiths.

The inscription helps us to reconstruct part of Cogidubnus' life story. He was probably a member of the family that ruled the Atrebates. After the Roman invasion in AD 43 the Romans appointed him king of this tribe, which was renamed the Regnenses. Cogidubnus was a faithful supporter of the Romans, and the kingship may have been a reward from the Emperor Claudius for helping them at the time of the invasion. He was granted the privilege of Roman citizenship and allowed to add two of the emperor's names (Tiberius Claudius) to his own.

He became a 'client king', which meant that he ruled on behalf of the emperor and that he was responsible for collecting the taxes and keeping the peace in his part of Britain. In this way he played an important part in keeping the southern region loyal to Rome, while the legions advanced to conquer the tribes in the north.

By dedicating the new temple to Neptune and Minerva rather than British gods, Cogidubnus publicly declared his loyalty to Rome. The temple was a reminder of Roman power. Its priests may well have been selected from the local British chieftains, many of whom were quick to see the advantages of supporting the new government. The inscription goes on to say that the temple was intended 'for the welfare of the Divine House'. By saying this, Cogidubnus is suggesting that the emperor himself is related to the gods and should be worshipped as such. The Romans encouraged the people of their empire to respect and worship the emperor in this way, because it helped to ensure obedience and to build up a sense of unity in a large empire that contained many tribes, many languages and many religions.

The Regnenses received not only a new king, but also a new capital town, Noviomagus. It was founded near the Sussex coast, where Chichester now stands (see the photograph on page 54). Three miles (five kilometres) to the west is the modern village of Fishbourne, where the remains of a large Roman building were found in 1960 by a workman digging a trench. During the eight years of excavation that followed, the archaeologists discovered that this was no ordinary country house. It was a palace as large and splendid as the fashionable houses in Rome itself, with one set of rooms after another, arranged round a huge courtyard. No inscription has been found to tell us who owned the palace, but it was so large, so magnificent and so near to Noviomagus that Cogidubnus seems the likeliest owner.

The palace, however, was not the first building erected on the site. The remains of earlier wooden buildings were found underneath it. These go back to the time of the Roman invasion, or very shortly afterwards. One of them was a granary. Pieces of metal and a helmet were also found nearby. These discoveries indicate the presence of soldiers; they may have been the soldiers of the Second Legion, commanded by Vespasian, a brilliant young general who led the attack against the Durotriges in the south-west. There was a harbour nearby, where Roman supply ships tied up. It is therefore likely that the Romans first used Fishbourne as a military port and depot where Vespasian assembled his troops.

In AD 69, Vespasian himself became emperor. A few years later, work began on the building of the palace at Fishbourne. Perhaps Vespasian was remembering the loyalty of Cogidubnus and was now presenting him with the palace in return for his continued support of the Romans.

As well as his native Celtic gods, Cogidubnus worshipped Roman ones: (from top) *Neptune and Minerva.*

Model of military store buildings at Fishbourne.

Vespasian and the Durotriges

Vespasian (inset) found the Durotriges defended by hill forts surrounded by huge banks and ditches, like Maiden Castle (above). Roundhouses filled the space inside the ditches. After the Roman victory, the defenders were buried by the fort entrance (left).

At Hod Hill, the Second Legion built a camp in the corner of the British hill fort.

Vocabulary checklist 15

agmen	column (of men), procession	**lītus**	sea-shore
alius	other, another	**mare**	sea
aqua	water	**miser**	miserable, wretched
claudō, claudere, clausī	shut, block	**nauta**	sailor
commodus	convenient	**prīnceps**	chief, chieftain
dēbeō, dēbēre, dēbuī	owe, ought	**quī**	who
equus	horse	**redeō, redīre, rediī**	return, go back
etiam	even	**sacerdōs**	priest
impediō, impedīre, impedīvī	delay, hinder	**teneō, tenēre, tenuī**	hold
lectus	couch	**unda**	wave
lentē	slowly	**vincō, vincere, vīcī**	win

A Roman arrowhead was found in the spine of one of the defenders of Maiden Castle.

IN AULA

STAGE 16

1 Cogidubnus Quīntum per aulam
dūcēbat. in aulā erant multae pictūrae,
quās pictor Graecus pīnxerat.

2 rēx iuvenem in hortum dūxit. in hortō
erant multī flōrēs, quōs Cogidubnus ex
Ītaliā importāverat.

3 tum ad ātrium vēnērunt. in mediō
ātriō erat fōns marmoreus, quī aquam
effundēbat.

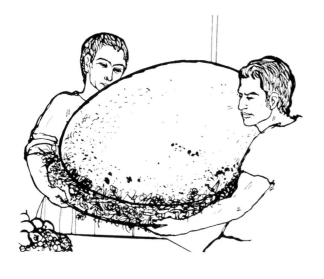

4 rēx et hospitēs in aulā cēnābant. cēna,
   quam coquī Graecī parāverant, optima
   erat. servī magnum ōvum in mēnsam
   posuērunt.

5 ex ōvō, quod servī in mēnsam
   posuerant, appāruit saltātrīx.

6 tum pūmiliōnēs, quōs rēx in Ītaliā
   ēmerat, intrāvērunt. pūmiliōnēs pilās
   iactābant.

Belimicus ultor

ultor *avenger*

Belimicus, prīnceps Canticus, postquam Dumnorix in certāmine
nāvālī vīcit, rem graviter ferēbat. īrātissimus erat. omnēs
hospitēs, quōs rēx ad aulam invītāverat, eum dērīdēbant. Canticī
quoque eum dērīdēbant et vituperābant. etiam servī, quī dē
naufragiō cognōverant, clam rīdēbant.   5

    'iste Dumnorix mē dēcēpit', Belimicus sibi dīxit. 'mē in
scopulum impulit et praemium iniūstē cēpit. decōrum est mihi
eum pūnīre.'

    Belimicus sēcum cōgitāvit et cōnsilium callidum cēpit. erant in
aulā multae bēstiae, quās rēx ē multīs terrīs importāverat. inter-   10
hās bēstiās erat ursa ingēns, quam servus Germānicus
custōdiēbat. Belimicus ad hunc servum adiit.

    'hoc animal est magnificum', inquit. 'mē valdē dēlectat. ursam
tractāre volō; eam nōn timeō.'

    itaque prīnceps ad ursam cotīdiē veniēbat; ursae cibum et   15
aquam dabat. paulātim ursam mānsuētam fēcit. tandem sōlus
ursam tractāre potuit.

    mox Cogidubnus cēnam et spectāculum nūntiāvit. amīcōs ad
aulam invītāvit. Belimicus statim ad servum Germānicum
contendit.   20

    'rēx hodiē spectāculum dat', inquit. 'hodiē hanc ursam in
aulam dūcere volō. nunc eam tractāre possum. hospitibus eam
ostendere volō.'

    servus invītus cōnsēnsit. Belimicus cachinnāns sibi dīxit,
    'parātus sum. nunc Dumnorigem pūnīre possum.'   25

graviter ferēbat *took badly*
dē naufragiō
  about the shipwreck
cognōverant: cognōscere
  find out, get to know
clam *secretly, in private*
impulit: impellere *push, force*
praemium *prize*
iniūstē *unfairly*
sēcum *to himself*
ursa *bear*
Germānicus *German*
adiit: adīre *approach, go up to*
tractāre *handle*
paulātim *gradually*
mānsuētam *tame*

pūmiliō

ursa

saltātrīx

Salvius et Quīntus prope rēgem recumbēbant.

rēx spectāculum dat

I

rēx cum multīs hospitibus in aulā cēnābat. Salvius et Quīntus
prope rēgem recumbēbant. Britannī cibum laudābant, Rōmānī
vīnum. omnēs hospitēs rēgī grātiās agēbant.

    subitō Belimicus tardus intrāvit.

    'ecce! naufragus noster intrat', clāmāvit Dumnorix. 'num tū
aliam nāvem āmīsistī?'.

    cēterī Belimicum dērīsērunt et Dumnorigī plausērunt.
Belimicus tamen Dumnorigī nihil respondit, sed tacitus
cōnsēdit.

    rēx hospitibus suīs spectāculum nūntiāvit. statim pūmiliōnēs
cum saltātrīcibus intrāvērunt et hospitēs dēlectāvērunt. deinde,
ubi rēx eīs signum dedit, omnēs exiērunt. Salvius, quem
pūmiliōnēs nōn dēlectāverant, clāmāvit,

    'haec cēna est bona. numquam cēnam meliōrem cōnsūmpsī.
sed ursam, quae saltat, vidēre volō. illa ursa mē multō magis
dēlectat quam pūmiliōnēs et saltātrīcēs.'

tardus	*late*
5 **naufragus**	*shipwrecked sailor*
tacitus	*silent, in silence*
cōnsēdit: cōnsīdere	*sit down*
10 **pūmiliōnēs: pūmiliō**	*dwarf*
cum saltātrīcibus	
	with dancing-girls
15 **saltat: saltāre**	*dance*
multō magis	*much more*

II

When you have read this part of the story, answer the questions on page 65.

rēx servīs signum dedit. servus Germānicus, quī hoc signum
exspectābat, statim cum ursā prōcessit et hospitibus eam
ostendit.

    Belimicus, simulatque hoc vīdit, surrēxit, et ad medium
triclīnium contendit.   5

    'mī Dumnorix!' clāmāvit. 'facile est tibi iocōs facere. sed ursam
tractāre nōn audēs! ego nōn timeō. ego, quem tū dērīdēs, ursam
tractāre audeō.'

    omnēs Belimicum spectābant attonitī. Belimicus, quī servum
iam dīmīserat, ursam ad Dumnorigem dūxit.   10

    'nōnne tū quoque ursam tractāre vīs?' rogāvit īnsolēns. 'nōnne
tū hospitibus spectāculum dare vīs?'

    Dumnorix impavidus statim surrēxit et Belimicum dērīsit.

    'facile est mihi', inquit, 'hanc ursam superāre. tē quoque,
homuncule, superāre possum.'   15

    tum cēterī, quī anteā timuerant, valdē cachinnāvērunt.
Belimicus, ubi cachinnōs audīvit, furēns ursam pulsāvit, et eam
ad Dumnorigem impulit. subitō ursa saeva sē vertit, et
Belimicum ferōciter percussit. tum prīncipēs perterritī clāmōrem
magnum sustulērunt et ad iānuās quam celerrimē cucurrērunt.   20
etiam inter sē pugnābant, quod exīre nōn poterant. ursa, quam
hic clāmor terruerat, ad lectum cucurrit, ubi rēx sedēbat.

    rēx tamen, quod claudicābat, effugere nōn poterat. Dumnorix
in ursam frūstrā sē coniēcit. Salvius immōtus stābat. sed Quīntus
hastam, quam servus Germānicus tenēbat, rapuit. hastam   25
celeriter ēmīsit et bēstiam saevam trānsfīxit. illa dēcidit mortua.

---

iocōs: iocus *joke*
audēs: audēre *dare*

homuncule: homunculus
   little man
cachinnāvērunt: cachinnāre
   roar with laughter
cachinnōs: cachinnus *laughter*
furēns *furious, in a rage*
saeva *savage*
sē vertit: sē vertere *turn round*

coniēcit: conicere *hurl, throw*
immōtus *still, motionless*
hastam: hasta *spear*
trānsfīxit: trānsfīgere *pierce*

Questions

		Marks
1	What did the German slave do at the king's signal?	2
2	What boast did Belimicus make (lines 7–8)? How did he show in lines 9–10 that he meant what he said?	2
3	What two challenges did Belimicus make to Dumnorix (lines 11–12)?	2
4	Look at lines 14–15. What two things did Dumnorix say that showed he was **impavidus** (line 13)?	2
5	What did Belimicus do when he heard the guests laughing at him (lines 17–18)?	2
6	What unexpected effect did this have on the bear? Give two details.	2
7	**perterritī**. How did the chieftains show that they were terrified (lines 19–20)?	2
8	Why did the guests fight among themselves?	1
9	Why did the bear run towards the king's couch?	1
10	Why could the king not escape?	1
11	In lines 23–6 how did each of the following people react?	
	a Dumnorix	1
	b Salvius	1
	c Quintus	3
12	What did their reactions show about each of their characters?	3

TOTAL **25**

Exotic animals and birds were collected from Africa and Asia and other parts of the ancient world. Some animals were destined for collections like that held by King Cogidubnus; others ended up being hunted and killed in the amphitheatre. This mosaic shows two ostriches being carried up the gangplank of a ship.

About the language: pluperfect tense

1   In this Stage, you have met examples of the pluperfect tense. They looked like this:

> in aulā erat ursa ingēns, quam rēx ex Ītaliā **importāverat**.
> *In the palace was a huge bear, which the king **had imported** from Italy.*

> sacerdōtēs, quī ad āram **prōcesserant**, victimās sacrificāvērunt.
> *The priests, who **had advanced** to the altar, sacrificed the victims.*

2   The complete pluperfect tense is as follows:

portāveram	*I had carried*	portāverāmus	*we had carried*
portāverās	*you (singular) had carried*	portāverātis	*you (plural) had carried*
portāverat	*s/he had carried*	portāverant	*they had carried*

3   Further examples:

    a   Rūfilla ancillās, quae cubiculum parāverant, laudāvit.
    b   in ātriō sedēbant hospitēs, quōs rēx ad aulam invītāverat.
    c   agricola nōs laudāvit, quod per tōtum diem labōrāverāmus.
    d   Belimicus, quī nāvem āmīserat, īrātissimus erat.
    e   Salvius mē pūnīvit, quod ē vīllā fūgeram.

4   Look at the differences between the present, perfect and pluperfect tenses:

	PRESENT	PERFECT	PLUPERFECT
first conjugation	portat *s/he carries*	portāvit *s/he carried*	portāverat *s/he had carried*
second conjugation	docet *s/he teaches*	docuit *s/he taught*	docuerat *s/he had taught*
third conjugation	trahit *s/he drags*	trāxit *s/he dragged*	trāxerat *s/he had dragged*
fourth conjugation	audit *s/he hears*	audīvit *s/he heard*	audīverat *s/he had heard*

5   Translate these further examples of third conjugation verbs.

    a   discēdit   discessit   discesserat
    b   scrībit   scrīpsit   scrīpserat
    c   facit   fēcit   fēcerat

Quīntus dē sē

postrīdiē Quīntus per hortum cum rēge ambulābat, flōrēsque
variōs spectābat. deinde rēx
  'quō modō', inquit, 'ex urbe Pompēiīs effūgistī? paterne et
māter superfuērunt?'
  Quīntus trīstis   5
  'periit pater', inquit. 'māter quoque in urbe periit. ego et ūnus
servus superfuimus. ad urbem Neāpolim vix effūgimus. ibi
servum, quī tam fortis et tam fidēlis fuerat, līberāvī.'
  'quid deinde fēcistī?' inquit rēx. 'pecūniam habēbās?'
  'omnēs vīllās, quās pater in Campāniā possēderat, vēndidī. ita   10
multam pecūniam comparāvī. tum ex Ītaliā discēdere voluī,
quod trīstissimus eram. ego igitur et lībertus meus nāvem
cōnscendimus.
  prīmō ad Graeciam vēnimus et in urbe Athēnīs habitābāmus.
haec urbs erat pulcherrima, sed cīvēs turbulentī. multī   15
philosophī, quī forum cotīdiē frequentābant, contrōversiās inter
sē habēbant.
  post paucōs mēnsēs, aliās urbēs vidēre voluimus. ad
Aegyptum igitur nāvigāvimus, et mox ad urbem Alexandrīam
advēnimus.'   20

variōs: varius *different*
quō modō *how*
superfuērunt: superesse
  survive

Neāpolim: Neāpolis *Naples*
vix *with difficulty*
tam *so*
fuerat *had been*
possēderat: possidēre *possess*
comparāvī: comparāre *obtain*
cōnscendimus: cōnscendere
  embark on, go on board
prīmō *first*
Athēnīs: Athēnae *Athens*
frequentābant: frequentāre
  crowd
mēnsēs: mēnsis *month*
Aegyptum: Aegyptus *Egypt*

*The Acropolis (or citadel) of Athens.
The prominent building is the
Parthenon, the temple of Athena
(whom the Romans called Minerva).*

Practising the language

1 Complete the verb in each relative clause by adding the right pluperfect ending. Then translate the sentence.

For example: fabrī, quōs imperātor mīs. . . . ., aulam aedificāvērunt.
fabrī, quōs imperātor **mīserat**, aulam aedificāvērunt.
The craftsmen, whom the emperor had sent, built the palace.

a   rēx, quī multōs hospitēs invītāv. . . . ., eīs cēnam optimam dedit.
b   prīncipēs, quī ex ātriō discess. . . . ., in āream prōcessērunt.
c   dōnum, quod ego rēgī ded. . . . ., pretiōsum erat.
d   ancillae, quae ad aulam vēn. . . . ., hospitēs dēlectāvērunt.
e   nōs, quī Belimicum cōnspex. . . . ., valdē rīsimus.
f   tū, quī ursam tractāv. . . . ., nōn timēbās.

The palace at Fishbourne

When the Roman soldiers moved on from Fishbourne, they left behind them a few buildings, some roads and a harbour. During the next thirty years many improvements were made. The roads were resurfaced and the drainage of this low-lying, rather marshy site was improved. The harbour was developed, and merchant ships called regularly. Work was begun on a guest house, and a fine new villa with a set of baths was built in the late sixties. This could have been a residence Cogidubnus built for himself on the outskirts of his new capital town.

But in about AD 75 everything changed. A vast area was cleared and levelled and the villa and baths became part of the south-east corner of a huge new building.

Specialist craftsmen were brought in from Italy: makers of mosaics, marble-workers, plasterers to make friezes, painters, carpenters, ironsmiths, hydraulic engineers to construct the fountains, and many others. All the construction and detailed manufacture was carried out on the site itself, where the builders lived and worked for many years. Many traces of the craftsmen's activity have been found. The floor of the area used by the stonemasons was littered with fragments of marble and coloured stone which had been imported from quarries in Italy, the Greek island of Scyros, Asia Minor and elsewhere. In another area were signs of iron-working where the smiths had manufactured door-hinges, handles and bolts.

The bath house (with the white roof) was incorporated into the later palace.

A Roman palace for a British king

The palace at Fishbourne was laid out in four long wings around a central garden.

The north wing contained three suites of rooms arranged around two internal courtyards where important guests could stay.

The hall was possibly used for religious purposes.

Visitors entered the palace through the entrance hall in the middle of the east wing. Some other rooms in this wing may have provided guest accommodation for less important visitors.

The west wing was built on a platform 1.5 metres higher than the rest of the palace. In the centre stood the audience chamber where the king received his subjects and interviewed officials; the other rooms may have been used as offices.

Today the south wing lies under a modern road and houses, but it may have been the accommodation for King Cogidubnus and his family, with a garden leading down from the verandah to the sea.

The bath house in the south-east corner is older than the rest of the building.

Elegant walls

The Romans' decorative schemes have been reconstructed from fragments.

One fragment of painted wall plaster from Fishbourne (left) is similar in style to a painting from Stabiae (right).

A frieze made of fine plaster and some of the marble pieces that decorated the walls (right).

Fashionable floors

Above and right: Cogidubnus' floors were covered with elegant black-and-white mosaics in geometric patterns. Try drawing the different shapes and work out how they fit together.

This floor, laid by a later owner, had a more complicated pattern. In the centre, Cupid rides a dolphin, and legendary sea creatures swim in the semi-circular spaces around.

The palace gardens

Like the palace, the garden was planned, laid out and decorated in the most fashionable Italian style. Whoever the owner was, he wanted his palace in Britain to look as Roman as possible.

The open area, which measured approximately 90 by 70 metres (100 by 80 yards), was laid out as a formal garden. The two lawns were not rolled and mown like a modern lawn, but the grass was kept short and tidy. Along the edges of the lawns archaeologists have found deep bedding trenches filled with a mixture of loam and crushed chalk where shrubs and flowers such as roses, flowering trees, box, rosemary, lilies and acanthus would probably have been planted.

Box hedges have been planted exactly where the Roman bedding trenches were found.

The reconstruction of the garden at Fishbourne features plants which Cogidubnus might have had in his garden. Clockwise from top left: acanthus, lily, rose, hyssop, grapevine.

A line of holes across the eastern side of the garden shows where wooden poles stood to support a trellis for climbing plants. These may have been rambler roses: the Romans were fond of roses and were good at growing them.

A broad path, 12 metres wide and surfaced with stone chippings, ran through the middle of the garden leading from the entrance hall to the audience chamber. Paths ran round the outside of the lawns, and a system of underground pipes brought water to the fountains which stood at intervals along the paths. Small marble and bronze statues were placed here and there to provide further decoration.

A slave working in the potting shed: a reconstruction at Fishbourne today.

Vocabulary checklist 16

aedificō, aedificāre, aedificāvī	build	nōnne?	surely?
auxilium	help	pereō, perīre, periī	die, perish
bonus	good	pōnō, pōnere, posuī	place, put
cōnsentiō, cōnsentīre, cōnsēnsī	agree	postrīdiē	on the next day
cōnsilium	plan, idea		
deinde	then	pūniō, pūnīre, pūnīvī	punish
dēlectō, dēlectāre, dēlectāvī	delight	simulac, simulatque	as soon as
effugiō, effugere, effūgī	escape	summus	highest, greatest, top
flōs	flower		
imperātor	emperor	tollō, tollere, sustulī	raise, lift up
inter	among	vertō, vertere, vertī	turn
ita	in this way		
melior	better		
nāvigō, nāvigāre, nāvigāvī	sail		

A detail from the Cupid and dolphin mosaic pictured on page 71, showing a sea-panther.

ALEXANDRIA

1 Alexandrīa magnum portum habet.
prope portum est īnsula. facile est
nāvibus ad portum pervenīre, quod in
hāc īnsulā est pharus ingēns. multae
nāvēs in portū Alexandrīae sunt.

2 Alexandrīa est urbs turbulenta. ingēns
turba semper urbem complet. multī
mercātōrēs per viās ambulant. multī
servī per urbem currunt. multī mīlitēs
per viās urbis prōcēdunt. mīlitēs
Rōmānī urbem custōdiunt.

3 postquam ad urbem pervēnimus,
templum vīdimus. ad hoc templum,
quod Augustus Caesar aedificāverat,
festīnāvimus. prō templō Caesaris erat
āra. ego vīnum in āram fūdī.

4 prope hanc urbem habitābat Barbillus,
vir dīves. Barbillus negōtium cum
patre meō saepe agēbat. vīllam
splendidam habēbat. ad vīllam Barbillī
mox pervēnī. facile erat mihi vīllam
invenīre, quod Barbillus erat vir
nōtissimus.

5 Barbillus multōs servōs habēbat, ego
nūllōs.
    'decōrum est tibi servum
Aegyptium habēre', inquit Barbillus.
    inter servōs Barbillī erat puer
Aegyptius. Barbillus, vir benignus,
mihi hunc puerum dedit.

tumultus

tumultus *riot*

I

in vīllā Barbillī diū habitābam. ad urbem cum servō quondam
contendī, quod Clēmentem vīsitāre volēbam. ille tabernam
prope portum Alexandrīae possidēbat. servus, quī mē dūcēbat,
erat puer Aegyptius.

in urbe erat ingēns multitūdō, quae viās complēbat.   5
mercātōrēs per viās ambulābant et negōtium inter sē agēbant.
fēminae et ancillae tabernās frequentābant; tabernāriī fēminīs et
ancillīs stolās ostendēbant. multī servī per viās urbis currēbant.
difficile erat nōbīs per viās ambulāre, quod maxima erat
multitūdō. tandem ad portum Alexandrīae pervēnimus. plūrimī   10
Aegyptiī aderant, sed nūllōs Graecōs vidēre poterāmus. puer,
postquam hoc sēnsit, anxius

'melius est nōbīs', inquit, 'ad vīllam Barbillī revenīre. ad
tabernam Clēmentis īre nōn possumus. viae sunt perīculōsae,
quod Aegyptiī īrātī sunt. omnēs Graecī ex hāc parte urbis   15
fūgērunt.'

'minimē!' puerō respondī. 'quamquam Aegyptiī sunt īrātī, ad
vīllam redīre nōlō. longum iter iam fēcimus. paene ad tabernam
Clēmentis pervēnimus. necesse est nōbīs cautē prōcēdere.'

quondam *one day, once*
ille *he*
tabernāriī: tabernārius
shopkeeper

plūrimī *very many*

sēnsit: sentīre *notice*
melius est *it would be better*

parte: pars *part*

II

*When you have read this part of the story, answer the questions
on page 79.*

itaque ad tabernam Clēmentis contendimus, sed in viā plūrimī
Aegyptiī nōbīs obstābant. in multitūdine Aegyptiōrum erat
senex, quī Graecōs Rōmānōsque vituperābat. omnēs eum intentē
audiēbant.

ubi hoc vīdī, sollicitus eram. puer Aegyptius, quī   5
sollicitūdinem meam sēnserat, mē ad casam proximam dūxit.

'domine, in hāc casā habitat faber, quī Barbillum bene nōvit.
necesse est nōbīs casam intrāre et perīculum vītāre.'

faber per fenestram casae forte spectābat. ubi puerum agnōvit,
nōs in casam suam libenter accēpit.   10

postquam casam intrāvimus, susurrāvī,
'quis est hic faber?'
'est Diogenēs, faber Graecus', respondit puer.

nōbīs obstābant
*were blocking our way, were
obstructing us*
sollicitūdinem: sollicitūdō
anxiety
casam: casa *small house*
nōvit *knows*
perīculum *danger*
fenestram: fenestra *window*
forte *by chance*
accēpit: accipere
take in, receive

ubi hoc audīvī, magis timēbam. nam in casā virī Graecī eram; extrā iānuam casae Aegyptiī Graecōs vituperābant. subitō servus clāmāvit, _15_

'ēheu! Aegyptiī īnfestī casam oppugnant.'

Diogenēs statim ad armārium contendit. in armāriō erant quīnque fūstēs, quōs Diogenēs extrāxit et nōbīs trādidit.

Aegyptiī iānuam effrēgērunt et in casam irrūpērunt. nōs _20_ Aegyptiīs fortiter resistēbāmus, sed illī erant multī, nōs paucī. septem Aegyptiī mē circumveniēbant. duōs graviter vulnerāvī, sed cēterī mē superāvērunt. prōcubuī exanimātus. ubi animum recēpī, casam circumspectāvī. fenestrae erant frāctae, casa dīrepta. Diogenēs in mediā casā stābat lacrimāns. prope mē _25_ iacēbat puer meus.

'puer mortuus est', inquit Diogenēs. 'Aegyptiī eum necāvērunt, quod ille tē dēfendēbat.'

magis _more_
extrā iānuam _outside the door_
īnfestī: īnfestus _hostile_
oppugnant: oppugnāre _attack_
effrēgērunt: effringere
break down
irrūpērunt: irrumpere _burst in_
septem _seven_
circumveniēbant:
circumvenīre _surround_
animum recēpī: animum
recipere
recover consciousness
dīrepta _pulled apart, ransacked_
dēfendēbat: dēfendere _defend_

Questions

		Marks
1	What was the old man doing? What was the crowd's reaction to him (lines 2–4)?	2
2	**ubi hoc vīdī, sollicitus eram** (line 5). Why do you think Quintus was worried?	1
3	**puer...mē ad casam proximam dūxit** (lines 5–7). Explain why the boy did this (lines 7–8).	2
4	Why were Quintus and the boy taken into the house (lines 9–10)?	2
5	**magis timēbam** (line 14). Why was Quintus more frightened now?	2
6	How did Diogenes prepare for the Egyptians' attack on the house?	2
7	How did the Egyptians get into the house (line 20)?	1
8	Why was it difficult to resist the Egyptians (lines 20–1)?	2
9	Describe the part Quintus played in the fight (lines 22–3).	3
10	Who was killed? Why do you think he was killed and not anyone else?	1+2

TOTAL **20**

About the language: genitive case

1   Study the following sentences:

        ad portum **Alexandrīae** mox pervēnimus.
        *We soon arrived at the harbour **of Alexandria**.*

        in vīllā **Barbillī** erant multī servī.
        *In the house **of Barbillus** were many slaves.*

        mīlitēs Rōmānī per viās **urbis** prōcēdēbant.
        *Roman soldiers were advancing through the streets **of the city**.*

        in multitūdine **Aegyptiōrum** erat senex.
        *In the crowd **of Egyptians** was an old man.*

The words in **bold type** are in the genitive case.

2   Compare the nominative singular with the genitive singular and
    genitive plural in each declension:

	first declension	*second declension*	*third declension*	
nominative singular	puella	servus	leō	cīvis
genitive singular	puellae	servī	leōnis	cīvis
genitive plural	puellārum	servōrum	leōnum	cīvium

3   Further examples:

a   multī servī in viā clāmābant. Quīntus per multitūdinem
     servōrum contendit.
b   Aegyptiī in casam fabrī ruērunt.
c   nūllī Graecī in illā parte urbis habitābant.
d   fēmina dīves magnum fundum habēbat. multī Aegyptiī in
     fundō fēminae labōrābant.
e   cīvēs viās complēbant. puer Quīntum per turbam cīvium
     dūxit.
f   mercātor togās in tabernā vēndēbat. iuvenēs et puerī ad
     tabernam mercātōris contendērunt.

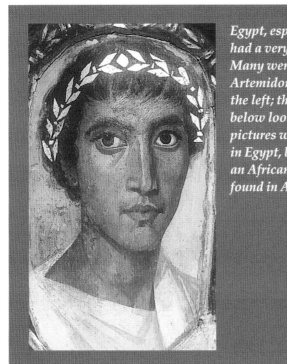

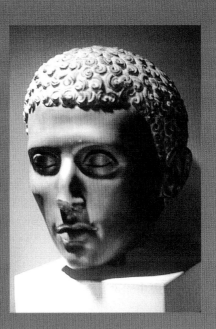

Egypt, especially Alexandria, had a very mixed population. Many were Greeks like Artemidorus in the portrait on the left; the unnamed man below looks Roman. These pictures were found elsewhere in Egypt, but the sculpture of an African man (right) was found in Alexandria itself.

ad templum

per viās urbis quondam cum Barbillō ībam. in multitūdine, quae viās complēbat, Aegyptiōs, Graecōs, Iūdaeōs, Syrōs vīdī. subitō vir quīdam nōbīs appropinquāvit. Barbillus, simulatque eum cōnspexit, magnum gemitum dedit.

Barbillus:	ēheu! quam miserī sumus! ecce Plancus, vir doctissimus, quī numquam tacet! semper dē templīs deōrum et dē aliīs monumentīs garrīre vult.	5
Plancus:	salvē, mī dulcissime! quid hodiē agis? quō contendis?	
Barbillus:	(*invītus*) ad templum.	10
Plancus:	ad templum Augustī?	
Barbillus:	minimē, ad templum Serāpidis īmus. nunc festīnāre dēbēmus, quod iter longum est. nōnne tū negōtium cum aliīs mercātōribus agere dēbēs? valē!	
Plancus:	hodiē ōtiōsus sum. commodum est mihi ad templum Serāpidis īre. dē Serāpide vōbīs nārrāre possum.	15

(Plancus nōbīscum ībat garriēns. nōbīs dē omnibus monumentīs nārrāre coepit.)

Barbillus:	(*susurrāns*) amīcus noster loquācior est quam psittacus et obstinātior quam asinus.

20

Iūdaeōs: Iūdaeī *Jews*
Syrōs: Syrī *Syrians*
vir quīdam *a certain man, someone*
gemitum: gemitus *groan*
doctissimus: doctus *learned, clever*
monumentīs: monumentum *monument*
garrīre *chatter, gossip*
mī dulcissime *my dear fellow*
quid … agis? *how are you?*

garriēns *chattering*
coepit *began*
susurrāns *whispering*
loquācior: loquāx *talkative*
psittacus *parrot*
obstinātior: obstinātus *obstinate, stubborn*

Plancus:	nunc ad templum Serāpidis advēnimus. spectāte	
	templum! quam magnificum! spectāte cellam!	
	statuam vīdistis, quae in cellā est? deus ibi cum	
	magnā dignitāte sedet. in capite deī est canistrum.	
	Serāpis enim est deus quī segetēs cūrat. opportūnē	25
	hūc vēnimus. hōra quārta est. nunc sacerdōtēs in ārā	
	sacrificium facere solent.	

(subitō tuba sonuit. sacerdōtēs ē cellā templī ad āram prōcessērunt.)

sacerdōs:	tacēte vōs omnēs, quī adestis! tacēte vōs, quī hoc	30
	sacrificium vidēre vultis!	

(omnēs virī fēminaeque statim tacuērunt.)

Barbillus:	*(rīdēns et susurrāns)* ehem! vidēsne Plancum? ubi	
	sacerdōs silentium poposcit, etiam ille dēnique	
	tacuit. mīrāculum est. deus nōs servāvit.	35

cellam: cella *sanctuary*
in capite *on the head*
canistrum *basket*
enim *for*
opportūnē *just at the right time*
hōra *hour*
quārta *fourth*
ārā: āra *altar*
facere solent
  are accustomed to make

rīdēns *laughing, smiling*
ehem! *well, well!*
silentium *silence*
dēnique *at last, finally*
mīrāculum *miracle*

Portrait of a priest of Serapis.

This sphinx marks the site of the temple of Serapis.

Left: *The god Serapis, with the corn measure on his head.*

Practising the language

1 Complete each sentence with the right form of the noun and then translate.

    a   in multitūdine . . . . stābat senex. (Aegyptiōrum, Aegyptiī)
    b   faber per fenestram . . . . spectābat. (casārum, casae)
    c   in viīs . . . . erant multī mercātōrēs. (urbis, urbium)
    d   domina per turbam . . . . festīnāvit. (ancillae, ancillārum)
    e   nōs ad templum Serāpidis pervēnimus. prō templō . . . . stābant multī cīvēs. (deī, deōrum)
    f   mercātōrēs vīllās splendidās habēbant. in vīllīs . . . . erant statuae pretiōsae. (mercātōris, mercātōrum)

2 Complete each sentence with the right form of the verb and then translate.

    a   ubi Diogenēs hoc dīxit, nōs casam . . . . (intrāvī, intrāvimus)
    b   Aegyptiī tabernam oppugnāvērunt, ubi vōs templum . . . . (vīsitābās, vīsitābātis)
    c   ego, ubi in urbe eram, tēcum negōtium . . . . (agēbam, agēbāmus)
    d   tū senem, quī Rōmānōs vituperābat, ... (audīvistī, audīvistis)
    e   nōs . . . ., quod sacerdōtēs ad āram prōcēdēbant. (tacēbāmus, tacēbam)
    f   vōs auxilium mihi semper . . . . (dabātis, dabās)
    g   pestis es! togās sordidās mihi . . . . (vēndidistis, vēndidistī)
    h   ad portum ambulābam. multōs mīlitēs Rōmānōs . . . . (vīdī, vīdimus)

3 Complete each sentence with the right verb from the box below and then translate.

volō	volumus	possum	possumus
vīs	vultis	potes	potestis
vult	volunt	potest	possunt

    a   māne ad portum ambulāre soleō, quod nāvēs spectāre . . . .
    b   mihi valdē placet puellam audīre, quae suāviter cantāre . . . .
    c   Barbille! nōnne dē monumentīs audīre . . . .?
    d   iter longum iam fēcistis; ad vīllam hodiē pervenīre nōn . . . .
    e   multī virī fēminaeque ad templum contendunt, quod sacrificium vidēre . . . .
    f   paucī sumus. Aegyptiōs superāre nōn . . . .
    g   māter, quae fīliō dōnum dare . . . ., togās in tabernā īnspicit.
    h   Aegyptiī fūstēs habent; Graecī eīs resistere nōn . . . .

Alexandria

Alexandria had three harbours. The Great Harbour and the Western Harbour lay on either side of a breakwater 1,200 metres (three-quarters of a mile) long which joined Pharos island to the mainland. The third harbour was on the large lake which lay behind the city and was connected by canals to the river Nile. From here goods were brought by a further canal, or overland, to the Red Sea; this was the route that led to India.

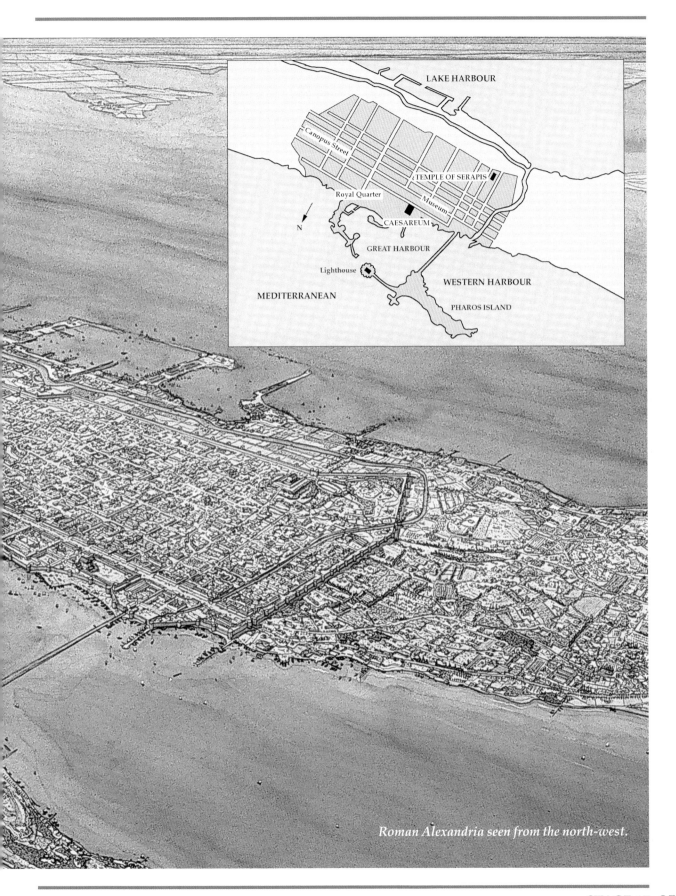

LAKE HARBOUR

Canopus Street

TEMPLE OF SERAPIS

Royal Quarter

Museum

N

CAESAREUM

GREAT HARBOUR

Lighthouse

WESTERN HARBOUR

MEDITERRANEAN

PHAROS ISLAND

Roman Alexandria seen from the north-west.

Alexandria

The site of this famous city was chosen by the Greek king, Alexander the Great, when he came to Egypt in 331 BC. Alexander noted both the excellent agricultural land and the fine harbour of a small fishing village west of the mouth of the Nile. Here there was good anchorage, a healthy climate and fresh water, and limestone quarries nearby to provide stone for building. He commanded his architect to plan and build a city which was to be a new centre of trade and civilisation.

Alexander died while the city was still developing, but the city was named after him and his body was later buried there in a magnificent tomb. He was succeeded as ruler by Ptolemy, one of his generals, whose descendants governed Alexandria and Egypt for the next three hundred years.

By the first century AD, when Egypt had become part of the Roman empire, Alexandria was probably as large and splendid as Rome itself; it was certainly the greatest city in the eastern part of the empire, with perhaps a million inhabitants. Much of its wealth and importance was due to its position. It stood at a meeting-place of great trade routes, and was therefore excellently placed for trading on a large scale. Merchants and businessmen were attracted to the city because it offered them safe harbours for their ships, a large number of dock-workers to handle their cargoes, huge warehouses for storage, and a busy market for buying and selling.

Into Alexandria came luxury goods such as bronze statues from Greece or fine Italian wines, and raw materials such as wood and marble to be used by craftsmen in the local workshops. Out to other countries went wheat in enormous quantities, papyrus, glassware and much else. A list in the *Red Sea Guide Book*, written by an Alexandrian merchant in the first century AD, gives some idea of the vast range of goods bought and sold in the city: 'clothes, cotton, skins, muslins, silks, brass, copper, iron, gold, silver, silver plate, tin, axes, adzes, glass,

Alexander the Great.

Coin of Alexandria, showing a ship passing the lighthouse.

The harbour today.

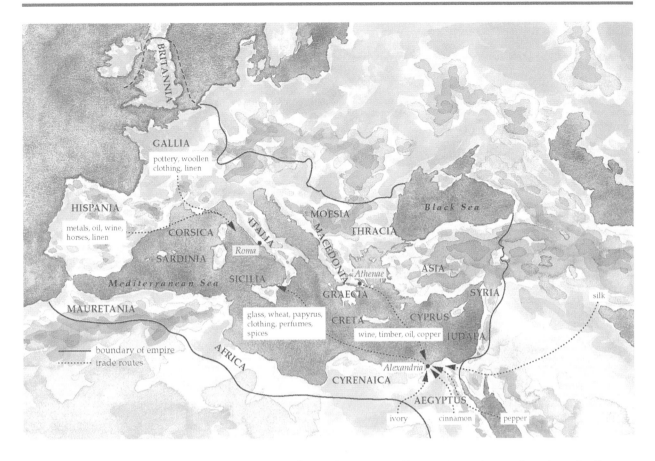

Within the map:

BRITANNIA

GALLIA
pottery, woollen clothing, linen

HISPANIA
metals, oil, wine, horses, linen

CORSICA

SARDINIA

ITALIA

Roma

SICILIA

MAURETANIA

MOESIA

THRACIA

MACEDONIA

Athenae

GRAECIA

CRETA

ASIA

Black Sea

SYRIA

CYPRUS

wine, timber, oil, copper

IUDAEA

silk

Mediterranean Sea

glass, wheat, papyrus, clothing, perfumes, spices

boundary of empire

trade routes

AFRICA

Alexandria

CYRENAICA

AEGYPTUS

ivory   cinnamon   pepper

Alexandria and trade in the first century AD.

ivory, tortoise shell, rhinoceros horn, wine, olive oil, sesame oil, rice, butter, honey, wheat, myrrh, frankincense, cinnamon, fragrant gums, papyrus.'

Travellers from Greece or Italy would approach Alexandria by sea. The first thing they would see, rising above the horizon, would be the huge lighthouse that stood on a little island called Pharos just outside the harbour. This lighthouse, which was itself called Pharos, was one of the seven wonders of the ancient world. It acted as a marker day and night for the thousands of ships that used the port each year.

Alexander's architect planned the city carefully, with its streets set out in a grid system, crossing each other at right angles as in many modern American cities. The main street, Canopus Street, was more than 30 metres (100 feet) wide, wider than any street in Rome and four times the size of any street that Quintus would have known in Pompeii. Some of the houses were several storeys high, and many of the public buildings were built of marble. By the Great Harbour was the Royal Quarter, an area of more than 260 hectares (one square mile) containing palaces, temples and gardens. West of the Royal Quarter was the Caesareum, where Quintus, in the paragraph on page 77, made his offering of wine. The Caesareum was a shrine begun by Queen Cleopatra in honour of the Roman

The Pharos

Right: *Model of the Pharos based on evidence like the coin on page 86, with a cut-away drawing.*
The Pharos was over 135 metres (440 feet) high, with a fire constantly alight at the top. A spiral ramp inside the lowest stage allowed fuel to be carried up by animals. Statues of Ptolemy II and his queen can be seen at the base of the lighthouse.

Below: *A 15th-century fort was built on the ruins of the Pharos.*

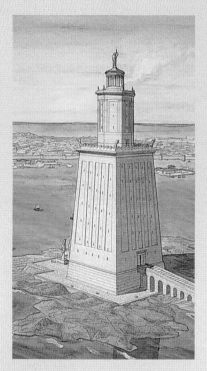
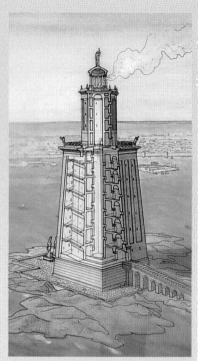

general Marcus Antonius and completed by the Emperor Augustus as a temple dedicated to himself. In the words of the Jewish writer Philo, it was 'wonderfully high and large, full of precious paintings and statues, and beautiful all over with gold and silver; it contains colonnades, libraries, courtyards and sacred groves, all made as skilfully as possible with no expense spared'.

In front of the Caesareum stood two obelisks, tall narrow pillars of granite, pointed at the top. They were brought from an ancient Egyptian temple and put in position by a Roman engineer in 13 BC. In the nineteenth century one was removed to London and placed on the embankment of the river Thames, and the other was taken to Central Park, New York. They are known as Cleopatra's Needles.

But Alexandria was more than a city of fine streets, glittering marble and busy trading; it was a centre of education and study. The university, known as the Museum and situated in the Royal Quarter, had the largest library in the ancient world with more than half a million volumes on its shelves. Professional scholars were employed to do research in a wide range of subjects – mathematics, astronomy, anatomy, geography, literature and languages. Here the first maps of the world were drawn, based on travellers' reports; here Euclid wrote his famous geometry textbook and Aristarchus put forward his theory that the Earth goes round the Sun.

Alexandria was a city of many different races, including Egyptians, Jews, Romans, Africans and Indians. But on the whole the people with most power and influence were the Greeks. They had planned the city and built it; they had ruled it before the Romans came and continued to play a part in running it under the Romans; theirs was the official language; they owned great wealth in Alexandria and enjoyed many privileges. This caused jealousy among the other races, and was one of the reasons why quarrels and riots frequently broke out. The Roman governor, or even the emperor himself, often had to step in and try to settle such disputes as fairly and peacefully as possible.

Right: *The Caesareum obelisks as they appeared at the end of the 18th century; in the bottom right hand corner you can see that one is lying on the ground, partially buried.*

Far right: *Cleopatra's Needle in London.*

After one violent riot involving the Jews, the Emperor Claudius included the following stern warning in a letter to the Alexandrians:

This mosaic floor comes from the dining-room of a rich Alexandrian. It shows the head of Medusa, which could turn those who looked at it to stone.

'Although I am very angry with those who stirred up the trouble, I am not going to enquire fully into who was responsible for the riot – I might have said, the war – with the Jews. But I tell you this, once and for all: if you do not stop quarrelling with each other, I shall be forced to show you what even a kind emperor can do when he has good reason to be angry.'

Underwater discoveries

Underwater excavations in the Great Harbour are now bringing much of the waterfront of ancient Alexandria back to life.

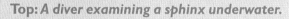

Top: *A diver examining a sphinx underwater.*

Above: *Raising part of a statue of one of the Greek rulers of Egypt, possibly Ptolemy II. The Pharos was completed in his reign.*

Right: *Several parts of the statue have been found, enabling it to be rebuilt. The huge figure, wearing the traditional royal dress of the Pharaohs, probably stood at the foot of the great lighthouse.*

Vocabulary checklist 17

Nouns in the checklists for Stages 17–20 are usually listed in the form of their nominative and genitive singular. Verbs are listed as before.

ā, ab	*from*	īnsula, īnsulae	*island*
animus, animī	*spirit, soul, mind*	invītus, invīta, invītum	*unwilling*
appropinquō, appropinquāre, appropinquāvī	*approach, come near to*	itaque	*and so*
		maximus	*very big*
		negōtium, negōtiī	*business*
āra, ārae	*altar*	numquam	*never*
bene	*well*	paucī	*few, a few*
benignus	*kind*	perveniō, pervenīre, pervēnī	*reach, arrive at*
diū	*for a long time*	quondam	*one day, once*
faber, fabrī	*craftsman*	recipiō, recipere, recēpī	*recover, take back*
facilis	*easy*		
graviter	*seriously*	resistō, resistere, restitī	*resist*
hūc	*here, to this place*		

Warships in a harbour. Wall painting from the temple of Isis at Pompeii.

EUTYCHUS ET CLEMENS

STAGE 18

Eutychus et Clēmēns

taberna

postquam ad urbem advēnimus, ego Clēmentī diū tabernam
quaerēbam. tandem Barbillus, quī trīgintā tabernās possidēbat,
mihi tabernam optimam obtulit. haec taberna prope templum
deae Īsidis erat. in hāc parte urbis via est, in quā omnēs
tabernāriī vitrum vēndunt. taberna, quam Barbillus mihi
offerēbat, optimum situm habēbat. Barbillus tamen dubitābat.

'sunt multī latrōnēs', inquit, 'in illā parte urbis. tabernāriī
latrōnēs timent, quod pecūniam extorquent et vim īnferunt.
latrōnēs lībertum meum interfēcērunt, quī nūper illam tabernam
tenēbat. eum in viā invēnimus mortuum. lībertus, quī senex
obstinātus erat, latrōnibus pecūniam dare nōluit. latrōnēs eum
necāvērunt tabernamque dīripuērunt.'

'Clēmēns vir fortis, nōn senex īnfirmus est', ego Barbillō
respondī. 'fortūna semper eī favet. hanc tabernam Clēmentī
emere volō. tibi centum aureōs offerō. placetne?'

'mihi placet', respondit Barbillus. 'centum aureī sufficiunt.'
Barbillō igitur centum aureōs trādidī.

5 **vitrum** *glass*
  situm: situs *position, site*
  dubitābat: dubitāre
    be doubtful
  latrōnēs: latrō *robber, thug*
10 **extorquent: extorquēre** *extort*
  vim īnferunt: vim īnferre
    use force, violence
  dīripuērunt: dīripere *ransack*
  īnfirmus *weak*
15 **fortūna** *fortune, luck*
  centum aureōs
    a hundred gold coins
  sufficiunt: sufficere *be enough*

latrōnēs eum necāvērunt.

in officīnā Eutychī

officīnā: officīna *workshop*

I

postquam tabernam Clēmentī dedī, ille mihi grātiās maximās
ēgit. statim ad viam, in quā taberna erat, festīnāvit: adeō
cupiēbat tabernam possidēre.

adeō *so much, so greatly*

    in viā vitreāriōrum erat ingēns turba. ibi Clēmēns tabernam
suam prope templum Īsidis cōnspexit. valvās ēvulsās vīdit,   5
tabernam dīreptam. īrātus igitur Clēmēns tabernārium vīcīnum
rogāvit,

in viā vitreāriōrum
   in the street of the glassmakers
valvās: valvae *doors*
ēvulsās: ēvulsus *wrenched off*
vīcīnum: vīcīnus
   neighbouring, nearby

    'quis hoc fēcit?'

    'rogā Eutychum!' inquit tabernārius, quī perterritus erat.

    Clēmēns statim Eutychum quaesīvit. facile erat Clēmentī eum   10
invenīre, quod officīnam maximam possidēbat. prō officīnā
Eutychī stābant quattuor servī Aegyptiī. Clēmēns numquam
hominēs ingentiōrēs quam illōs Aegyptiōs vīderat. eōs tamen
nōn timēbat. ūnum servum ex ōrdine trāxit.

prō officīnā
   in front of the workshop
quattuor *four*

    'heus! Atlās!' inquit Clēmēns. 'num dormīs? Eutychum,   15
dominum tuum, interrogāre volō. cūr mihi obstās? nōn decōrum
est tibi lībertō obstāre.'

interrogāre *question*

    tum Clēmēns servōs attonitōs praeteriit, et officīnam Eutychī
intrāvit.

praeteriit: praeterīre *go past*

II

Eutychus in lectō recumbēbat; cibum ē canistrō gustābat. valdē
sūdābat, et manūs in capillīs servī tergēbat. postquam
Clēmentem vīdit,

sūdābat: sūdāre *sweat*
manūs … tergēbat
   was wiping his hands

    'quis es, homuncule?' inquit. 'quis tē hūc admīsit? quid vīs?'

    'Quīntus Caecilius Clēmēns sum', respondit Clēmēns. 'dē   5
tabernā, quam latrōnēs dīripuērunt, cognōscere volō. nam illa
taberna nunc mea est.'

capillīs: capillī *hair*
admīsit: admittere *let in*

    Eutychus, postquam hoc audīvit, Clēmentem amīcissimē
salūtāvit, et eum per officīnam dūxit. ipse Clēmentī fabrōs suōs
dēmōnstrāvit. in officīnā trīgintā vitreāriī Aegyptiī dīligenter   10
labōrābant; aderat vīlicus, quī virgam vibrābat.

amīcissimē: amīcē
   in a friendly way

    Eutychus, postquam Clēmentī officīnam ostendit, negōtium
agere coepit.

    'perīculōsum est, mī amīce, in viā vitreāriōrum', inquit. 'multī
fūrēs ad hanc viam veniunt, multī latrōnēs. omnēs igitur   15
tabernāriī auxilium ā mē petunt. tabernāriī mihi pecūniam dant,
ego eīs praesidium. tabernam tuam servāre possum. omnēs
tabernāriī mihi decem aureōs quotannīs dare solent. paulum est.
num tū praesidium meum recūsāre vīs?'

praesidium *protection*
paulum *little*

Clēmēns tamen Eutychō nōn crēdēbat.   20
  'ego ipse tabernam, in quā habitō, servāre possum', inquit
Clēmēns. 'praesidium tuum recūsō.'
  tum lībertus sēcūrus exiit.

sēcūrus *without a care*

Alexandria, home of luxury glass

*Alexandrian glass was traded widely, even outside
the Roman Empire. The glass beaker on the right was
made in Alexandria but was found in Afghanistan. It
has a painted design showing the princess Europa
being carried off on the back of a bull, which is
Jupiter in disguise.*

*The disc below is carved from glass in two layers,
white on blue. We do not know where it was made,
but the technique was probably used in Alexandria.*

Clēmēns tabernārius

When you have read this story, answer the questions on page 99.

Clēmēns mox tabernam suam renovāvit. fabrōs condūxit, quī
valvās mūrōsque refēcērunt. cēterī tabernāriī, quamquam
Eutychum valdē timēbant, Clēmentem libenter adiuvābant. nam
Clēmēns cōmis erat et eīs saepe auxilium dabat.

haec taberna, ut dīxī, prope templum deae Īsidis erat. ad hoc   5
templum Clēmēns, quī pius erat, cotīdiē adībat. ibi deam Īsidem
adōrābat et eī ōrnāmentum vitreum saepe cōnsecrābat.

sacerdōtēs, quī templum administrābant, mox Clēmentem
cognōvērunt. deinde Clēmēns Īsiacīs sē coniūnxit. sacerdōtēs eī
librum sacrum dedērunt, in quō dē mystēriīs deae legere   10
poterat. Clēmēns in templō cum sacerdōtibus cēnāre solēbat. in
cellā templī habitābat fēlēs sacra. Clēmēns eam semper
mulcēbat, et eī semper aliquid ex paterā suā dabat.

mox plūrimōs amīcōs Clēmēns habēbat. nam tabernāriī, quī
Eutychō pecūniam invītī dabant, paulātim Clēmentī   15
cōnfīdēbant. tabernāriī Eutychum inimīcum putābant,
Clēmentem vindicem. tandem omnēs Eutychō pecūniam trādere
nōluērunt.

renovāvit: renovāre *restore*
condūxit: condūcere *hire*
refēcērunt: reficere *repair*
ut *as*
pius *respectful to the gods*
adōrābat: adōrāre *worship*
ōrnāmentum *ornament*
vitreum: vitreus
   glass, made of glass
cōnsecrābat: cōnsecrāre
   dedicate
Īsiacīs: Īsiacus *follower of Isis*
sē coniūnxit: sē coniungere
   join
sacrum: sacer *sacred*
mystēriīs: mystēria
   mysteries, secret worship
mulcēbat: mulcēre *stroke*
paterā: patera *bowl*
cōnfīdēbant: cōnfīdere *trust*
putābant: putāre *think*
vindicem: vindex
   champion, defender

itaque Eutychus latrōnēs collēgit et eīs fūstēs dedit.

'iste Clēmēns', inquit Eutychus, 'molestissimus est. necesse est 20
eī poenās dare.'

latrōnēs, postquam fūstēs cēpērunt, ad tabernam Clēmentis
contendērunt.

collēgit: colligere
gather, collect
poenās dare
pay the penalty, be punished

Questions

		Marks
1	How did Clemens get his shop repaired?	2
2	Why did the other shopkeepers help Clemens (lines 2–4)?	2
3	Where was Clemens' shop? Why was this convenient for Clemens (lines 5–6)?	2
4	How did he show his respect for the goddess (lines 6–7)?	2
5	How did the priests help Clemens to learn more about the goddess (lines 9–11)?	2
6	Where did the sacred cat live? In what ways did Clemens show kindness to it?	1 + 2
7	**mox plūrimōs amīcōs Clēmēns habēbat** (line 14). Who were these friends?	1
8	From line 16, pick out the Latin word that shows how Clemens' friends regarded Eutychus. How did they finally oppose Eutychus?	2
9	What conclusion did Eutychus come to about Clemens (lines 20–1)? Give two details.	2
10	Read the last sentence. Suggest two things the thugs might do.	2
	TOTAL	20

About the language: gender

1   You have already seen how an adjective changes its ending to
    agree, in case and number, with the noun it describes. For
    example:

    ACCUSATIVE SINGULAR: rēx nūntium **fortem** salūtāvit.
                            The king greeted the brave messenger.

    NOMINATIVE PLURAL: mercātōrēs **fessī** dormiēbant.
                            The tired merchants were sleeping.

2   An adjective agrees with the noun it describes not only in case and
    number but also in a third way, gender. All nouns in Latin belong
    to one of three genders: masculine, feminine and neuter.
    Compare the following sentences:

        Clēmēns amīcōs **callidōs** laudāvit.
        Clemens praised the clever friends.

        Clēmēns ancillās **callidās** laudāvit.
        Clemens praised the clever slave-girls.

    In both sentences, the word for 'clever' is accusative plural. But in
    the first sentence, the masculine form **callidōs** is used, because it
    describes **amīcōs**, which is masculine; in the second sentence, the
    feminine form **callidās** is used, because it describes **ancillās**, which
    is feminine.

3   The forms of the adjective which you have met are listed on
    page 153 in the Language Information section.

Detail of a mosaic panel, including coloured glass pieces.

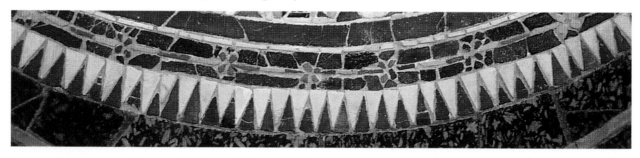

4 Further examples:

a 'ubi est coquus novus?' rogāvit Barbillus.
b 'ubi est templum novum?' rogāvit Quīntus.
c magnae nāvēs ad portum Alexandrīae nāvigābant.
d tabernāriī ignāvī per fenestrās spectābant.
e nūntius dominō crūdēlī epistulam trādidit.
f mīlitēs latrōnem in vīllā mercātōris Graecī invēnērunt.

Write down the Latin noun and adjective pair in each sentence and use the Vocabulary in the Language Information section to find the gender of each noun and adjective pair.

5 The Latin word for 'who' or 'which' at the beginning of a relative clause changes like an adjective to match the gender of the word it describes. Notice how the forms of **quī** (masculine), **quae** (feminine) and **quod** (neuter) are used in the following examples:

> rēx, **quī** in aulā habitābat, caerimōniam nūntiāvit.
> *The king, who lived in the palace, announced a ceremony.*

> puella, **quae** per forum contendēbat, latrōnēs vīdit.
> *The girl, who was hurrying through the forum, saw the thugs.*

> dōnum, **quod** āthlētam valdē dēlectāvit, erat statua.
> *The gift, which pleased the athlete very much, was a statue.*

6 Nouns such as **pater**, **fīlius**, **sacerdōs**, which refer to males, are usually masculine; nouns such as **māter**, **fīlia**, **uxor**, which refer to females, are usually feminine. Other nouns can be masculine (e.g. **hortus**), feminine (e.g. **nāvis**) or neuter (e.g. **nōmen**).

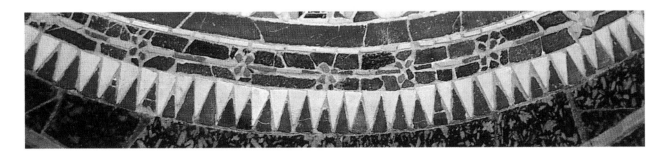

prō tabernā Clēmentis

Clēmēns in templō deae Īsidis cum cēterīs Īsiacīs saepe cēnābat.
quondam, ubi ā templō, in quō cēnāverat, domum redībat,
amīcum cōnspexit accurrentem.

'taberna ardet! taberna tua ardet!' clāmāvit amīcus. 'tabernam
tuam dīripiunt Eutychus et latrōnēs. eōs vīdī valvās ēvellentēs,   5
vitrum frangentēs, tabernam incendentēs. fuge! fuge ex urbe!
Eutychus tē interficere vult. nēmō eī latrōnibusque resistere
potest.'

Clēmēns tamen nōn fūgit, sed ad tabernam quam celerrimē
contendit. postquam illūc advēnit, prō tabernā stābat immōtus.   10
valvās ēvulsās, tabernam dīreptam vīdit. Eutychus extrā
tabernam cum latrōnibus Aegyptiīs stābat, rīdēbatque. Eutychus
cachinnāns

'mī dulcissime!' inquit. 'nōnne tē dē hāc viā monuī? nōnne
amīcōs habēs quōs vocāre potes? cūr absunt? fortasse   15
sapientiōrēs sunt quam tū.'

Clēmēns cum summā tranquillitāte eī respondit,
'absunt amīcī, sed deī mē servāre possunt. deī hominēs
scelestōs pūnīre solent.'

Eutychus īrātissimus   20
'quid dīcis?' inquit. 'tūne mihi ita dīcere audēs?'

tum Eutychus latrōnibus signum dedit. statim quattuor
Aegyptiī cum fūstibus Clēmentī appropinquābant. Clēmēns
cōnstitit. via, in quā stābat, erat dēserta. tabernāriī perterritī per
valvās tabernārum spectābant. omnēs invītī Clēmentem   25
dēseruerant, simulatque Eutychus et latrōnēs advēnērunt.

subitō fēlēs sacra, quam Clēmēns mulcēre solēbat, ē templō
exiit. Clēmentem rēctā petīvit. in umerum Clēmentis īnsiluit.
omnēs Aegyptiī statim fūstēs abiēcērunt et ad pedēs Clēmentis
prōcubuērunt. Clēmentem, quem fēlēs sacra servābat, laedere   30
nōn audēbant.

saeviēbat Eutychus, sīcut taurus īrātus. tum fēlēs in
Eutychum īnsiluit, et caput vehementer rāsit.

'melius est tibi fugere', inquit Clēmēns.

Eutychus cum latrōnibus perterritus fūgit. posteā neque   35
Clēmentem neque tabernāriōs laedere temptābat. nunc
Clēmēns est prīnceps tabernāriōrum.

domum: domus *home*
accurrentem: accurrēns
   running up
ēvellentēs: ēvellēns
   wrenching off
frangentēs: frangēns *breaking*
incendentēs: incendēns
   burning, setting on fire
illūc *there, to that place*

monuī: monēre *warn*

 sapientiōrēs: sapiēns *wise*
tranquillitāte: tranquillitās
   calmness
scelestōs: scelestus *wicked*

dēseruerant: dēserere *desert*
rēctā *directly, straight*
īnsiluit: īnsilīre
   jump onto, jump into
abiēcērunt: abicere
   throw away
laedere *harm*
sīcut taurus *like a bull*
rāsit: rādere *scratch*
neque … neque *neither… nor*
temptābat: temptāre *try*

Egyptian Cats

The Egyptians kept cats both as pets and to control rats and mice in their granaries and food stores. They also venerated cats as sacred animals as they thought they were earthly forms of the goddess Isis and another goddess called Bastet. When cats died they were mummified; vast numbers of them have been excavated.

Left: *This expensive bronze cat was made as an offering to the goddess Bastet around 600 BC.*

In Egyptian legend, each night a cat kills an evil snake that tries to prevent the sun from rising.

Practising the language

1   Complete each sentence with the right form of the adjective and then translate. Remember that adjectives agree with nouns in case, number and gender. If you are unsure of the gender of a noun you can check it in the vocabulary at the back of the book.

    a   .... tabernāriī Eutychō pecūniam dedērunt. (multī, multae)
    b   latrōnēs senem .... necāvērunt. (obstinātum, obstinātam)
    c   Quīntus templum .... vīsitāvit. (magnificam, magnificum)
    d   Aegyptiī Graecōs .... petīvērunt. (perterritōs, perterritās)
    e   faber .... ad casam mē invītāvit. (benignus, benigna)
    f   mercātor lībertō .... praemium obtulit. (fidēlī, fidēlibus)
    g   Eutychus officīnam .... habēbat. (ingentem, ingēns)
    h   servus ē vīllā dominī .... fūgit. (crudēlem, crudēlis)

2   Complete each sentence with the right noun or phrase and then translate.

    a   ...., quam Clēmēns possidēbat, in viā vitreāriōrum erat. (taberna, tabernae)
    b   ...., quī templum administrābant, Clēmentī librum
        sacrum dedērunt. (sacerdōtēs, sacerdōs)
    c   in templō, quod prope tabernam Clēmentis erat, habitābat
        .... (fēlēs sacra, fēlēs sacrae)
    d   ubi Eutychus et latrōnēs advēnērunt,
        .... valdē timēbant. (tabernārius Graecus, cēterī tabernāriī)
    e   .... ad templum Īsidis festīnāvit et Clēmentī
        dē tabernā nārrāvit. (amīcus fidēlis, amīcī Graecī)
    f   .... ē templō Īsidis celeriter discessērunt et
        ad tabernam cucurrērunt. (amīcus fidēlis, duo amīcī)

3   Complete each sentence with the right form of the verb and then translate.

    a   Clēmēns ad tabernam, quam Quīntus ...., festīnāvit. (ēmerat, ēmerant)
    b   ingēns turba, quae viam ...., tabernam
        spectābat. (complēverat, complēverant)
    c   Clēmēns ad Eutychum, quī latrōnēs ....,
        contendit. (mīserat, mīserant)
    d   Eutychus Clēmentem, quem servī nōn ....,
        amīcissimē salūtāvit. (terruerat, terruerant)
    e   Eutychus dē tabernāriīs, quī praesidium ....,
        Clēmentī nārrāvit. (petīverat, petīverant)
    f   Clēmēns tamen praesidium, quod Eutychus eī ....,
        recūsāvit. (obtulerat, obtulerant)

Pick out the Latin word for 'who' or 'which' (**quī**, **quae**, etc.) at the beginning of each relative clause. Which noun does it refer to? Write down the gender of each pair.

Glassmaking in Alexandria

In the stories in this Stage, Quintus establishes Clemens in one of Alexandria's oldest and most successful industries – glassmaking. The earliest Egyptian glass vessels, discovered in tombs, date from about 1500 BC. When Alexandria was founded in 331 BC, craftsmen of many kinds soon flocked to the city, keen to practise and improve their skills. Among these craftsmen were glassmakers, who experimented with various ways of making glass, producing a wide range of different shapes and colours. Before long their styles and methods were being copied all over the civilised world. Their skills quickly spread to Rome, where there was a big demand for Alexandrian glass, and from Rome to Gaul, to the Rhineland and to Britain.

Glass is made from sand, with the addition of sodium carbonate produced from the ash of certain plants. Its earliest use was for glazing pottery. As time went on, it was discovered – perhaps by a potter – that if glass is heated until it becomes semi-liquid, it can be shaped and left to harden. At first this shaping was carried out by wrapping the molten glass round a clay and sand core, which had been moulded into the shape of a vase or any other object that was required. When the glass had hardened, the core was scraped out or washed out. But this method was only suitable for making small vessels, such as perfume containers.

A scent-bottle made around a sand core.

This bowl was made by lining a mould with differently coloured sticks of glass, then heating them until they melted and fused together.

This bowl is decorated in a typical Alexandrian style known as 'millefiori' (Italian for 'a thousand flowers'). Small pieces of coloured glass were arranged in a mould and then heated until they fused together.

Gradually, the craftsmen learned to make glass in various colours by adding different chemicals. Blue, green, brown and white were the commonest colours for the basic shapes, but many other colours were used for decoration. This was often added by trailing thin lines of molten glass onto the finished vessel, rather like piping coloured icing onto a fancy cake.

Late in the first century BC, in Egypt or Syria, a new invention completely changed the glassmaking industry. The glassmakers discovered that instead of wrapping the molten glass round a core, they could pick it up on the end of a hollow pipe, and shape it by blowing down the pipe. Glass-blowing is illustrated in the drawing below. The workman in the background has

A modern glass-blower.

dipped his pipe into the crucible above the furnace and has lifted out a blob of molten glass. His next job is to blow steadily down the pipe, as the workman at the front of the picture is doing, in order to shape the glass into a hollow bubble. By careful reheating and repeated blowing, the glass bubble can be made very big. Many different shapes can be produced by swinging the bubble gently during the blowing, or by using special tools for shaping and cutting, some of which are shown in the picture. Identical objects can be produced by blowing the glass into a mould. Handles, bases and decoration can then be added; for example, thin lines of molten glass can be trailed onto the vessel.

After the invention of glass-blowing, glassmakers were able to produce many different shapes and sizes of vessel quickly and efficiently. From then on, glass could be used not only for making luxury goods but for producing large quantities of ordinary household objects for everyday use. The fame of Alexandrian glass spread, and the Alexandrian glassmakers prospered.

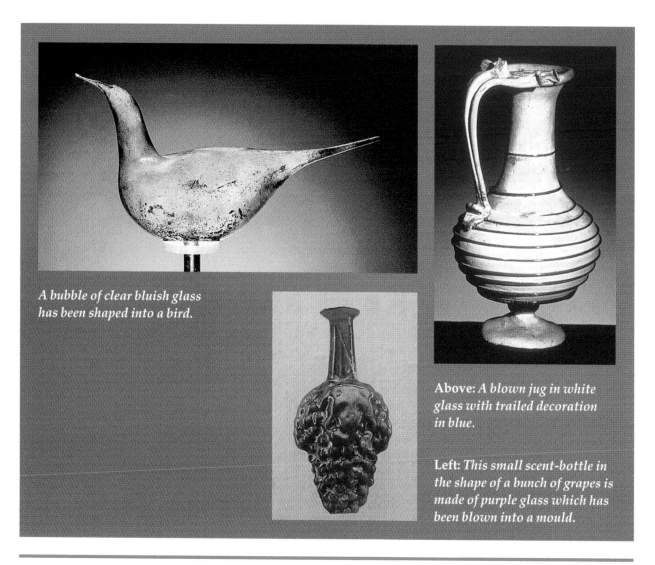

A bubble of clear bluish glass has been shaped into a bird.

Above: *A blown jug in white glass with trailed decoration in blue.*

Left: *This small scent-bottle in the shape of a bunch of grapes is made of purple glass which has been blown into a mould.*

The Nile. Notice the fertile agricultural land between the desert and the river.

Egypt

South of Alexandria stretched the fertile valley of the river Nile. Every year the Nile flooded, watering the land and depositing rich new soil on the fields. This produced not only enough corn to supply the whole of Egypt but also a large surplus to be exported. However, the profits from the corn trade benefited only a small number of people.

Before the Romans came to Egypt, the country had been ruled by Egyptian 'pharaohs' (kings), then by Persians and Greeks. These rulers had worked out a system for making the fullest possible use of the land for their own advantage. They regarded the whole country as their own property, and treated the peasant farmers as their private force of workers. They had drawn up a detailed register of all the plots of land in Egypt and the crops grown on them, and in every village lived government officials whose job was to keep the register up-to-date and check up on the peasants who worked on the land.

The peasants had no choice but to work hard all the year round. They were not allowed to leave their village without permission, they had to plant whatever crop they were told, and they did not receive their share of the harvest until the ruler had received his. They were also responsible for the upkeep and repair of the country's canals and dykes. Everything the peasants did was checked by the officials. The following certificate, for example, was issued by an official called Dioscurus:

Peasants harvesting corn under supervision.

Everything the peasants did was checked by the officials.

'Certificate. Year 16 of the Emperor Caesar Traianus Hadrianus Augustus. Zoilus son of Petesuchus son of Elites, his mother being Taorsenuphis, has worked on the embankment operations for four days at the canal of Patsontis in Bacchias. I, Dioscurus, signed this.'

Such careful supervision gave the peasants little chance of going unnoticed or avoiding work. All they could do was complain. Many letters have been found addressed by peasants to government officials, and they frequently say the same thing: 'We are worn out: we shall run away'.

When the Romans came, they did nothing to improve the life of the peasants. The certificate quoted above was issued in the reign of the Emperor Hadrian, more than a hundred and fifty years after the Romans' arrival in Egypt. Like the previous rulers, the Romans were more concerned to use the land for their own benefit than to improve the working conditions of peasant farmers. Above all, they wanted to ensure a steady supply of corn to Rome. Without the corn from Egypt and North Africa, the huge population of Rome would have starved and rioted. To avoid this danger the emperors made sure that Egypt was under their personal control.

Further money was needed by the government, for example, to maintain the Pharos, the police and the huge numbers of officials. This money was raised by taxation. There were taxes, for example, on vineyards, slaves, dovecotes, and imported and exported goods. Government officials checked continually on the day-to-day activities of the Egyptians. If a man went fishing, an official went with him to register his catch; if anyone sailed out of Alexandria without a permit, he might be fined one third of his property. Licences were required for such activities as brewing, beekeeping and pig-breeding.

Under these conditions, it is not surprising that bribery and corruption were common. Here is an extract from the private accounts kept by a Greek living in Egypt:

Part of an Egyptian official document. This papyrus was written in Greek during the Roman period of rule, and concerns work done on a canal.

gift	240 drachmas
to the guard	20 drachmas
bribes	2,200 drachmas
to two police agents	100 drachmas
to Hermias, police agent	100 drachmas
to a soldier	500 drachmas

Although such payments were illegal, they were regarded as a normal part of daily life, and the government usually ignored them.

The god of the Nile bearing the river's rich harvest.

Vocabulary checklist 18

audeō, audēre	*dare*	**mīles, mīlitis**	*soldier*
caput, capitis	*head*	**nam**	*for*
coepī	*I began*	**nēmō**	*no one*
cognōscō, cognōscere, cognōvī	*get to know, find out*	**obstō, obstāre, obstitī**	*obstruct, block the way*
dea, deae	*goddess*	**pars, partis**	*part*
dēmōnstrō, dēmōnstrāre, dēmōnstrāvī	*point out, show*	**petō, petere, petīvī**	*beg for, ask for*
discēdō, discēdere, discessī	*depart, leave*	**posteā**	*afterwards*
		prō	*in front of*
fortasse	*perhaps*	**quō?**	*where? where to?*
ibi	*there*	**recūsō, recūsāre, recūsāvī**	*refuse*
libenter	*gladly*	**soleō, solēre**	*be accustomed*
manus, manūs	*hand*		

A Roman mosaic uses millefiori glass pieces for the clothes of these Egyptian characters.

ISIS

STAGE 19

1 hic vir est Aristō. Aristō est amīcus Barbillī. in vīllā splendidā habitat, sed miserrimus est.

2 haec fēmina est Galatēa. Galatēa est uxor Aristōnis. Galatēa marītum saepe vituperat, numquam laudat.

3 haec puella est Helena. Helena est fīlia Aristōnis et Galatēae. multī iuvenēs hanc puellam amant, quod pulcherrima est.

4 pompa splendida per viās Alexandrīae
prōcēdit. omnēs Alexandrīnī hanc
pompam spectāre volunt.

5 hī virī sunt sacerdōtēs deae Īsidis. Aristō
hōs virōs intentē spectat. sacerdōtēs
statuam deae per viās portant.

6 hae puellae prō pompā currunt. Helena
hās puellās intentē spectat. puellae
corōnās rosārum gerunt.

7 pompa ad templum Serāpidis advenit.
prope hoc templum stant duo iuvenēs. hī
iuvenēs tamen pompam nōn spectant.

Aristō

Aristō vir miserrimus est, quod vītam dūram vīvit. pater
Aristōnis scrīptor nōtissimus erat, quī in Graeciā habitābat.
tragoediās optimās scrībēbat. Aristō, quod ipse tragoediās
scrībere vult, vītam quiētam quaerit; sed uxor et fīlia eī obstant.

Galatēa, uxor Aristōnis, amīcōs ad vīllam semper invītat. 5
amīcī Galatēae sunt tībīcinēs et citharoedī. hī amīcī in vīllā
Aristōnis semper cantant et iocōs faciunt. Aristō amīcōs uxōris
semper fugit.

Helena quoque, fīlia Aristōnis et Galatēae, patrem vexat.
multōs iuvenēs ad vīllam patris invītat. amīcī Helenae sunt 10
poētae. in vīllā Aristōnis poētae versūs suōs recitant. Aristō hōs
versūs nōn amat, quod scurrīlēs sunt. saepe poētae inter sē
pugnant. saepe Aristō amīcōs fīliae ē vīllā expellit. difficile est
Aristōnī tragoediās scrībere.

dūram: dūrus *hard, harsh*
vīvit: vīvere *live*
scrīptor *writer*
tragoediās: tragoedia *tragedy*

tībīcinēs: tībīcen *pipe player*
citharoedī: citharoedus
 cithara player

amat: amāre *love, like*
expellit: expellere *throw out*

*The Roman theatre at
Alexandria.*

A writer of plays.

diēs fēstus

diēs fēstus *festival, holiday*

I

cīvēs laetī erant. nam hiems erat cōnfecta. iam prīmus diēs vēris
erat. iam sacerdōtēs deam Īsidem per viās urbis ad portum ferre
solēbant. pompa, quam plūrimī Alexandrīnī spectāre volēbant,
splendida erat.

    hanc pompam tamen Barbillus spectāre nōlēbat.   5

    'nōn commodum est mihi hodiē ad urbem īre', inquit. 'ego
hanc pompam saepe vīdī, tū tamen numquam. amīcus meus
igitur, Aristō, tē ad pompam dūcere vult.'

    Barbillō grātiās ēgī, et cum Aristōne ad portum ībam. Galatēa
et fīlia, Helena, nōbīscum ībant. viās urbis iam complēbant cīvēs   *10*
Alexandrīnī. ubi portuī appropinquābāmus, Galatēa fīliam et
marītum assiduē vituperābat:

    'Helena! nōlī festīnāre! tolle caput! Aristō! ēmovē hanc
turbam! turba Alexandrīnōrum tōtam viam complet. in magnō
perīculō sumus.'   *15*

cōnfecta: cōnfectus *finished*
vēris: vēr *spring*
Alexandrīnī: Alexandrīnus
    Alexandrian

assiduē *continually*
tolle! *hold up!*

This portrait of a young woman called Eirene ('Peace') might help us to picture Helena in our stories. Portraits like this, and those on the next two pages, used to be attached to Egyptian mummies during the Roman period. They enable us to visualise the varied faces in the Alexandrian crowd at the festival of Isis.

II

When you have read this part of the story, answer the questions on page 117.

postquam ad templum Augustī vēnimus, Galatēa
  'locum optimum nōvimus', inquit, 'unde tōtum spectāculum
vidēre solēmus. servus nōbīs illum locum servat. Aristō! nōnne
servum māne ēmīsistī?'
  'ēheu!' Aristō sibi dīxit.   5
  ubi ad illum locum, quem Galatēa ēlēgerat, tandem
pervēnimus, Galatēa duōs iuvenēs cōnspexit. hī iuvenēs locum
tenēbant, ubi Galatēa stāre volēbat.
  'marīte!' exclāmāvit. 'ēmovē illōs iuvenēs! ubi est servus
noster? nōnne servum ēmīsistī?'   10
  'cārissima', respondit Aristō, quī anxius circumspectābat,
'melius est nōbīs locum novum quaerere. iste servus sānē
neglegēns erat.'
  Galatēa tamen, quae iam īrātissima erat, Aristōnem incitāvit.
ille igitur iuvenibus appropinquāvit et cōmiter locum poscēbat. 15
uxor tamen vehementer clāmāvit,
  'iuvenēs! cēdite! nōlīte nōbīs obstāre!'
  iuvenēs, quamquam rem graviter ferēbant, cessērunt. iuvenēs
Galatēam spectābant timidī, Helenam avidī.
  subitō spectātōrēs pompam cōnspexērunt. statim multitūdō 20
spectātōrum clāmōrem sustulit.
  'ecce pompa! ecce! dea Īsis!'

unde *from where*

sānē *obviously*

cōmiter *politely, courteously*

avidī: avidus *eager*

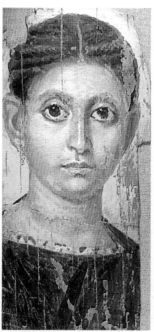

Questions

		Marks
1	**ad templum Augustī vēnimus**. Write down one thing you already know about this temple.	1
2	**locum optimum nōvimus** (line 2). Why did Galatea describe the place as **optimum**?	1
3	What was the slave's job?	1
4	Why do you think Aristo said '**ēheu!**' to himself?	2
5	In lines 6–8, what unpleasant surprise did Galatea have?	1
6	What did Galatea tell her husband to do? What suspicion did she have (lines 9–10)?	2
7	What alternative suggestion did Aristo make? How did he try to avoid blame?	2
8	After going up to the young men, how did Aristo carry out his wife's instruction?	1
9	What did Galatea do that showed her attitude was different from her husband's? What did she tell the young men to do (line 17)?	1 + 2
10	Why do you think they finally gave up the place (lines 18–19)?	2
11	Why do you think Galatea at last stopped nagging everyone?	1
12	Having read this part of the story, how would you describe Aristo's character? Make three points and give evidence for each one.	3

TOTAL **20**

About the language 1: hic and ille

1   You have now met the following forms of the Latin word for 'this'
    (plural 'these'):

	SINGULAR			PLURAL	
	masculine	*feminine*	*neuter*	*masculine*	*feminine*
nominative	hic	haec	hoc	hī	hae
accusative	hunc	hanc	hoc	hōs	hās

hic vir est Barbillus.	*This man is Barbillus.*
hanc pompam vīdī.	*I saw this procession.*
hae stolae sunt sordidae!	*These dresses are dirty!*
tibi **hōs** flōrēs trādō.	*I hand these flowers to you.*

2   You have also met the following forms of the Latin word for 'that'
    (plural 'those'):

	SINGULAR			PLURAL	
	masculine	*feminine*	*neuter*	*masculine*	*feminine*
nominative	ille	illa	illud	illī	illae
accusative	illum	illam	illud	illōs	illās

illa fēmina est Galatēa.	*That woman is Galatea.*
Clēmēns **illōs** sacerdōtēs saepe adiuvābat.	*Clemens often used to help those priests.*
illae viae sunt perīculōsae.	*Those roads are dangerous.*
multī Aegyptiī **illud** templum vīsitābant.	*Many Egyptians used to visit that temple.*

3   Note that **hic** and **ille** agree in case, number and gender with the
    nouns they describe.

4   Further examples:

   a   haec cēna est optima.
   b   latrōnēs illum mercātōrem vituperant.
   c   hoc templum prope forum est.
   d   hī servī sunt Aegyptiī.
   e   illud monumentum nōtissimum est.
   f   ille iuvenis puellās vexat.

pompa

pompa adveniēbat. prō pompā currēbant multae puellae, quae flōrēs in viam spargēbant. post multitūdinem puellārum tubicinēs et puerī prōcēdēbant. puerī suāviter cantābant. tubicinēs tubās īnflābant. nōs, quī pompam plānē vidēre poterāmus, assiduē plaudēbāmus. duo iuvenēs tamen, quōs Galatēa ē locō ēmōverat, pompam vidēre vix poterant.

5

spargēbant: **spargere** *scatter*
tubicinēs: **tubicen** *trumpeter*
īnflābant: **īnflāre** *blow*
plānē *clearly*

Helena:	spectā illās rosās, quās fēminae in viam spargunt! rosās pulchriōrēs quam illās numquam vīdī.
iuvenis prīmus:	pompam vidēre nōn possum. sed spectā illam puellam! puellam pulchriōrem quam illam rārō vīdī.
Galatēa:	Helena! hūc venī! stā prope mē! Aristō! cūr fīliam tuam in tantā multitūdine nōn cūrās?

rosās: **rosa** *rose*

10

rārō *rarely*

<table>
<tr><td></td><td>(subitō omnēs tubicinēs tubās vehementer
īnflābant.)</td><td>15</td><td></td></tr>
<tr><td>Galatēa:</td><td>ō mē miseram! ō caput meum! audīte illōs
tubicinēs! audīte illum sonitum! quam
raucus est sonitus tubārum!</td><td></td><td>**sonitum: sonitus** *sound*
raucus *harsh*</td></tr>
<tr><td>iuvenis secundus:</td><td>tubicinēs vix audīre possum. quam raucae
sunt vōcēs fēminārum Graecārum!</td><td>20</td><td>**vōcēs: vōx** *voice*</td></tr>
<tr><td></td><td>(post turbam puerōrum tubicinumque vēnit dea
ipsa. quattuor sacerdōtēs effigiem deae in umerīs
ferēbant.)</td><td></td><td></td></tr>
<tr><td>Galatēa:</td><td>spectā illam stolam! pulcherrima est illa
stola, pretiōsissima quoque. ēheu! vīlēs sunt
omnēs stolae meae, quod marītus avārus
est.</td><td>25</td><td>**vīlēs: vīlis** *cheap*</td></tr>
<tr><td></td><td>(subitō iuvenēs, quī effigiem vidēre nōn
poterant, Galatēam trūsērunt. iuvenis forte
pedem Galatēae calcāvit.)</td><td>30</td><td>**trūsērunt: trūdere** *push, shove*
calcāvit: calcāre *tread on*</td></tr>
<tr><td></td><td>ō iuvenem pessimum! nōlī mē vexāre! nōn
decōrum est mātrōnam trūdere. num bēstia
es?</td><td></td><td>**mātrōnam: mātrōna** *lady*</td></tr>
<tr><td>Helena:</td><td>māter! hic iuvenis forte tibi nocuit.
spectātōrēs nōs premunt, quod pompam
vidēre cupiunt.</td><td>35</td><td>**nocuit: nocēre** *hurt*
premunt: premere *push*</td></tr>
<tr><td>Galatēa:</td><td>Helena! nōlī istum iuvenem dēfendere!
īnsolentissimus est. Aristō! cūr mē nōn
servās? uxōrem fīliamque numquam cūrās.
miserrima sum!</td><td>40</td><td></td></tr>
<tr><td>Aristō:</td><td>ēheu! uxor mē vexat, fīlia mātrem. clāmōrēs
eārum numquam effugere possum. facile
est mihi tragoediās scrībere. tōta vīta mea
est tragoedia.</td><td>45</td><td>**eārum** *their*</td></tr>
</table>

tōta vīta mea est tragoedia!

About the language 2: imperatives

1 In each of the following sentences, one or more people are being told to do something:

> māter! **spectā** pompam! māter! pater! **spectāte** pompam!
> *Mother! Look at the procession!* *Mother! Father! Look at the procession!*

> Helena! **venī** ad mē! servī! **venīte** ad mē!
> *Helena! Come to me!* *Slaves! Come to me!*

The form of the verb in **bold type** is known as the imperative. If only one person is being told to do something, the imperative singular is used; if more than one person, the imperative plural is used.

2 Compare the imperative forms with the infinitive:

	IMPERATIVE		INFINITIVE
	SINGULAR	PLURAL	
first conjugation	portā!	portāte!	portāre
	carry!	*carry!*	*to carry*
second conjugation	docē!	docēte!	docēre
	teach!	*teach!*	*to teach*
third conjugation	trahe!	trahite!	trahere
	drag!	*drag!*	*to drag*
fourth conjugation	audī!	audīte!	audīre
	listen!	*listen!*	*to listen*

3 Study the way in which people are ordered **not** to do things:

SINGULAR nōlī currere! *don't run!*
  nōlī cantāre! *don't sing!*

PLURAL nōlīte festīnāre! *don't hurry!*
  nōlīte trūdere! *don't push!*

nōlī and **nōlīte** are the imperative forms of the verb **nōlō**. Notice that they are used with the infinitive. **nōlī currere** literally means 'be unwilling to run' and so 'don't run'.

4 Further examples:

a iuvenēs! tacēte! e nōlī dormīre!
b dīligenter labōrā! f nōlīte discēdere!
c date mihi pecūniam! g nōlīte Rōmānōs interficere!
d mē adiuvā! h nōlī mē pūnīre!

In each example, state whether the order is given to one person or more than one.

hodiē sōl Arietī appropinquat. *According to legend, the heavens were supported on the shoulders of a giant, Atlas. In this sculpture of Atlas carrying the globe of the heavens, the constellation Aries (the Ram) can be seen towards the left, across three narrow parallel lines that mark the path of the sun across the heavens.*

vēnātiō

I

Barbillus mē et Aristōnem ad vēnātiōnem invītāvit. māne
vīlicum Phormiōnem cum multīs servīs ēmīsit. Phormiō sēcum
duōs haedōs dūxit. sed, ubi ē vīllā discēdēbāmus, astrologus
Barbillī commōtus ad nōs cucurrit.

    'domine, quō festīnās?' clāmāvit. 'cūr ē vīllā hodiē exīre vīs?'   5

    'ad praedium meum iter facimus', Barbillus astrologō
respondit.

    'sed, domine', inquit astrologus, 'immemor es. perīculōsum
est tibi hodiē ē vīllā exīre, quod hodiē sōl Arietī appropinquat.'

    ubi hoc audīvī, astrologum dērīsī. Barbillus, quamquam eī   10
crēdēbat, mē offendere nōluit. postquam rem diū cōgitāvit,

    'mihi placet exīre', inquit.

    astrologus igitur, ubi dominō persuādēre nōn potuit,
amulētum eī dedit. tum sēcūrī ad praedium Barbillī
contendimus. per partem praediī flūmen Nīlus lēniter fluēbat.   15

    ubi illūc advēnimus, multōs servōs vīdimus collēctōs. in hāc
multitūdine servōrum erant nōnnūllī Aethiopes, quī hastās in
manibus tenēbant. prope Aethiopas stābat Phormiō, vīlicus
Barbillī.

    Phormiō 'salvē, domine!' inquit. 'omnēs rēs tibi parāvimus.   20
scaphās, quās postulāvistī, comparāvimus.'

    'haedōs cecīdistis?' rogāvit Barbillus.

    'duōs haedōs cecīdimus, domine', respondit vīlicus. 'eōs in
scaphās iam posuimus.'

haedōs: haedus
    kid, young goat
astrologus *astrologer*
commōtus *alarmed, excited*
praedium *estate*
immemor *forgetful*
Arietī: Ariēs
    the Ram (sign of the zodiac)
offendere *displease*

persuādēre *persuade*
amulētum *amulet, lucky charm*
flūmen Nīlus *river Nile*
lēniter *gently*
collēctōs: collēctus *assembled*
Aethiopes *Ethiopians*

scaphās: scapha
    punt, small boat
cecīdistis: caedere *kill*

II

tum Phormiō nōs ad rīpam flūminis dūxit, ubi scaphae, quās comparāverat, dēligātae erant. postquam scaphās cōnscendimus, ad palūdem, in quā crocodīlī latēbant, cautē nāvigāvimus. ubi mediae palūdī appropinquābāmus, Barbillus Phormiōnī signum dedit. haedōs Phormiō in aquam iniēcit. crocodīlī, ubi haedōs cōnspexērunt, praecipitēs eōs petēbant. tum Aethiopes crocodīlōs agitāre coepērunt. hastās ēmittēbant et crocodīlōs interficiēbant. magna erat fortitūdō crocodīlōrum, maior tamen perītia Aethiopum. mox multī crocodīlī mortuī erant.

subitō ingentem clāmōrem audīvimus.

'domine!' clāmāvit Phormiō. 'hippopotamus, quem Aethiopes ē palūde excitāvērunt, scapham Barbillī ēvertit. Barbillum et trēs servōs in aquam dēiēcit.'

quamquam ad Barbillum et ad servōs, quī in aquā natābant, celeriter nāvigāvimus, crocodīlī iam eōs circumvēnerant. hastās in crocodīlōs statim ēmīsimus. ubi crocodīlōs dēpulimus, Barbillum et ūnum servum servāre potuimus. sed postquam Barbillum ex aquā trāximus, eum invēnimus vulnerātum. hasta, quam servus ēmīserat, umerum Barbillī percusserat. Barbillus ā servō suō graviter vulnerātus erat.

rīpam: rīpa *bank*
dēligātae: dēligātus *tied up, moored*
palūdem: palūs *marsh, swamp*
crocodīlī: crocodīlus *crocodile*
iniēcit: inicere *throw in*
praecipitēs: praeceps *headlong*
fortitūdō *courage*
perītia *skill*
hippopotamus *hippopotamus*
ēvertit: ēvertere *overturn*
dēpulimus: dēpellere *drive off*
ā servō suō *by his own slave*

Above: *An amulet, in the form of the hippopotamus god Thueris.*

Left: *A mosaic showing pygmies hunting a crocodile and hippos in the river Nile.*

About the language 3: vocative case

1   In each of the following sentences, somebody is being spoken to:

Aristō! quam stultus es!   *Aristo! How stupid you are!*
quid accidit, **Barbille**?   *What happened, Barbillus?*
contendite, **amīcī**!   *Hurry, friends!*
cūr rīdētis, **cīvēs**?   *Why are you laughing, citizens?*

The words in **bold type** are in the vocative case. If only one person is spoken to, the vocative singular is used; if more than one person, the vocative plural is used.

2   The vocative case has the same form as the nominative with the exception of the vocative singular of words in the second declension.

3   Compare the nominative singular and vocative singular of second declension nouns like **servus** and **Salvius**:

nominative	*vocative*
servus labōrat.	cūr labōrās, **serve**?
amīcus gladium habet.	dā mihi gladium, **amīce**!
Eutychus est in viā.	ubi sunt latrōnēs, **Eutyche**?
Salvius est īrātus.	quid accidit, **Salvī**?
fīlius currit.	cūr curris, **fīlī**?
Holcōnius in lectō recumbit.	**Holcōnī**! surge!

4   The vocative plural has the same form as the nominative plural:

nominative	*vocative*
custōdēs dormiunt.	vōs semper dormītis, **custōdēs**.
puerī in forō stant.	ubi est theātrum, **puerī**?
puellae ad pompam festīnant.	nōlīte currere, **puellae**!

A Nile crocodile in a painting in the temple of Isis at Pompeii.

Practising the language

1   Complete each sentence with the right form of **hic** or **ille** and then translate. If you are not sure of the gender of a noun check it in the vocabulary at the end of the book.

a   . . . . astrologus Barbillō dē perīculō
    persuādēre nōn potuit. (hic, hoc)
b   Phormiō . . . . servōs ad flūmen Nīlum
    mīsit. (illōs, illās)
c   . . . . flūmen est perīculōsum. (hic, hoc)
d   . . . . servī prope flūmen stābant. (hī, hae)
e   Phormiō . . . . scaphās in rīpā īnstrūxit. (illōs, illās)
f   . . . . crocodīlī haedōs petīvērunt. (illī, illae)
g   Aethiopes . . . . hippopotamum
    ē palūde excitāvērunt. (illum, illam, illud)
h   . . . . hasta umerum Barbillī
    percussit. (hic, haec, hoc)

2   Using the table of nouns on pages 150–1 of the Language Information section, complete these sentences by filling in the endings, and then translate. For example:

       mercātor in viā stābat. amīcī mercātōr... salūtāvērunt.
       mercātor in viā stābat. amīcī **mercātōrem** salūtāvērunt.
       A merchant was standing in the street. The friends greeted the merchant.

a   puella stolam habēbat. stola puell... erat splendidissima.
b   servus leōn... in silvā vīdit. leō dormiēbat.
c   puellae tabernam intrāvērunt. mercātor puell... multās stolās
    ostendit.
d   cīvēs rēgem laudāvērunt, quod rēx cīv... magnum
    spectāculum dederat.
e   serv..., quod dominum timēbant, fūgērunt.
f   multī cīvēs in casīs habitābant. casae cīv... erant sordidae.
g   servī dīligenter labōrāvērunt. serv... igitur praemium dedī.
h   puer perterritus ad templum cucurrit et iānuam templ...
    pulsāvit.
i   rē..., quī in aulā sedēbat, tubam audīvit.
j   Salvius puer..., quī amphorās portābant, vehementer
    vituperāvit.

The worship of Isis

Isis was one of Egypt's oldest and most important goddesses. The Egyptians worshipped Isis for her power to give new life. They believed that she was responsible for the new life which followed the annual flooding of the Nile waters, and that she offered a hope of life after death for those who became her followers.

One of the most important festivals of Isis was held at the beginning of spring. It took place annually on 5 March, when the sailing season began and the large grain ships, so crucial to Rome's food supply, could once again set off safely across the Mediterranean. A statue of Isis was carried in a procession down to the Great Harbour.

The procession was headed by dancers and musicians playing pipes, trumpets and castanets. Female attendants scattered roses in the roadway and over the tightly packed crowd. The statue of Isis was carried high on the shoulders of her priests, so that everyone could get a glimpse of the goddess and her splendid robe. Next came more priests and more trumpeters and finally the high priest, wearing garlands of roses and shaking a sacred rattle known as a **sistrum**.

At the harbour, a special newly built ship was moored. Its stern was shaped like a goose's neck and was covered with gold plate. First the high priest dedicated the ship to Isis and offered prayers; then the priests and people loaded it with gifts of spices and flowers; finally the mooring-ropes were unfastened and the wind carried the ship out to sea.

After the ceremony at the harbour, the statue of Isis was taken back to the temple. The spectators crowded into the open area in front of the temple, and the priests replaced the statue in the **cella** or sanctuary. Then a priest read to the people from a sacred book, and recited prayers for the safety of the Roman people and their emperor, and for sailors and ships.

Isis

According to the Egyptians, Isis loved her brother, the god Osiris who appeared on earth in the form of a man. However, Osiris was murdered. His body was cut up and the pieces were scattered throughout the world. Overcome with grief, Isis set out on a search for the pieces of Osiris' corpse. When at last she had found them all, a miracle took place: the dead Osiris was given new life and became the father of the child Horus. This is why the Egyptians worshipped Isis as a bringer of new life.

Isis nursing her child, Horus.

Two bronze sistra.

Woman holding a sistrum.

Above: *Isis, as the protector of shipping, holds a square sail in this Alexandrian coin. The Pharos can be seen on the right.*

Left: *Isis and her brother Osiris.*

Left: *Mosaic showing the Nile in flood. The Egyptians believed that Isis sent these floods, which brought Egypt its fertile soil.*

The festival was noisy and colourful. Everybody was on holiday, and although the religious ceremony was serious, it was also good entertainment. When the ceremony was over, the Alexandrians continued to enjoy themselves. Their behaviour was sometimes criticised, for example by the writer Philo:

'They give themselves up to heavy drinking, noisy music, amusements, feasting, luxury and rowdy behaviour, eager for what is shameful and neglecting what is decent. They wake by night and sleep by day, turning the laws of nature upside down.'

But in spite of Philo's words, a festival of Isis was not just an excuse for a holiday. The worship of the goddess was taken seriously by many Egyptians, who went regularly to her temple, prayed to her statue and made offerings. Some of them, like Clemens in Stage 18, went further and became members of the special brotherhood of Isis. This involved a long period of preparation leading up to an initiation ceremony in the temple. Those who wished to join the brotherhood of Isis had to begin with an act of repentance for the sins they had committed in the past; for example, they might offer a sacrifice, or abstain from food, or go on a pilgrimage. In a Latin novel known as *The Golden Ass*, the main character becomes a follower of Isis. He explains to his readers how he prepared to be admitted to the brotherhood. First his body was washed by the priests in a ceremony of baptism; next he was taught about the sacred mysteries of the goddess, and forbidden to reveal them to anyone outside the brotherhood; then he fasted for ten days before finally undergoing the initiation ceremony in the temple.

A ceremony outside a temple of Isis.

As the worship of Isis spread from Egypt into the Greek and Roman world, new ways were found of depicting the goddess, left. This Egyptian drawing shows her with her hieroglyph, a throne, above her head. She carries a sceptre in one hand and an ankh, the symbol for life, in the other. On the right is a Roman painting of Isis holding the sacred cobra of Egypt. It was found in her temple at Pompeii.

This was a ceremony of mystery and magic, full of strange and emotional experiences for the worshippers. Those who were initiated believed that they had personally met Isis and that by dedicating themselves to her they could hope for life after death. But the exact details of the ceremony were kept strictly secret, as the narrator of *The Golden Ass* explains: 'If you are interested in my story, you may want to know what was said and done in the temple. I would tell you if I was allowed to tell, you would learn if you were allowed to hear; but your ears and my tongue would suffer for your foolish curiosity.'

The worship of Isis spread from Alexandria across the ancient world. Temples to Isis have been found in places as far apart as London and the Black Sea. A group of priests serving in a temple of Isis at Pompeii suffered a miserable death when the city was destroyed in the eruption of Vesuvius. They collected the sacred objects and treasures, and fled from the temple, but by then it was too late. Their bodies were found along the route of their flight across the city, each corpse surrounded by the valuables he had tried to save.

This food – nuts, grain and bread – was found in the temple of Isis at Pompeii.

Vocabulary checklist 19

Adjectives from now on are usually listed as in the Language Information section (see page 170).

amō, amāre, amāvī	*love, like*	**iter, itineris**	*journey*
cārus, cāra, cārum	*dear*	**locus, locī**	*place*
cōgitō, cōgitāre,		**māne**	*in the morning*
cōgitāvī	*think,*	**nōvī**	*I know*
	consider	**perīculum,**	
comparō, comparāre,		**perīculī**	*danger*
comparāvī	*obtain*	**plūrimī**	*very many*
cōnficiō, cōnficere,		**poscō, poscere,**	
cōnfēcī	*finish*	**poposcī**	*demand, ask for*
cūrō, cūrāre, cūrāvī	*look after*	**tot**	*so many*
fīlia, fīliae	*daughter*	**vexō, vexāre,**	
fluō, fluere, flūxī	*flow*	**vexāvī**	*annoy*
forte	*by chance*	**vīvō, vīvere,**	
grātiās agō	*I thank, give*	**vīxī**	*live*
	thanks	**vix**	*hardly,*
hasta, hastae	*spear*		*scarcely*
illūc	*there, to that place*	**vōx, vōcis**	*voice*

In Egyptian mythology, the male hippo was identified with Seth, the god of storms and the enemy of Isis and Osiris. Small figures like this are often found in tombs.

MEDICUS

STAGE 20

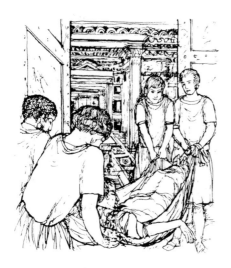

1 servī ad vīllam revēnērunt, Barbillum portantēs.

2 ancillae prope lectum stābant, lacrimantēs.

3 astrologus in cubiculum irrūpit, clāmāns.

4 Barbillus, in lectō recumbēns, astrologum audīvit.

5 Phormiō ad urbem contendit, medicum quaerēns.

remedium astrologī

ego et servī cum Barbillō ad vīllam quam celerrimē rediimus.
multus sanguis ex vulnere Barbillī effluēbat. Phormiō, quī servōs
vulnerātōs sānāre solēbat, tunicam suam sciderat; partem
tunicae circum umerum Barbillī dēligāverat. fluēbat tamen
sanguis.

    servī, quī Barbillum portābant, ubi cubiculum intrāvērunt, in
lectum eum lēniter posuērunt. duae ancillae prope lectum
stābant lacrimantēs. Phormiō ancillās ē cubiculō ēmīsit et servōs
ad sē vocāvit.

    'necesse est vōbīs', inquit, 'magnum numerum arāneārum
quaerere. ubi sanguis effluit, nihil melius est quam arāneae.'

    servī per tōtam vīllam contendēbant, arāneās quaerentēs;
magnum clāmōrem tollēbant. Phormiō, postquam servī multās
arāneās ad cubiculum tulērunt, in umerum dominī eās
collocāvit.

    astrologus ancillās lacrimantēs vīdit, servōsque clāmantēs
audīvit. statim in cubiculum Barbillī irrūpit, exclāmāns:

    'nōnne hoc prōvīdī? ō nefāstum diem! ō dominum īnfēlīcem!'

    'habēsne remedium?' rogāvī anxius.

    'remedium certum habeō', respondit astrologus. 'facile est
mihi Barbillum sānāre, quod nōs astrologī sumus vērī medicī.
prīmō necesse est mihi mūrem nigrum capere. deinde mūrem
captum dissecāre volō. postrēmō eum in umerum Barbillī
pōnere volō. hoc sōlum remedium est.'

    subitō, Barbillus, quī astrologum audīverat, oculōs aperuit.
postquam mihi signum languidum dedit, in aurem meam
susurrāvit,

    'quaere Petrōnem, medicum bonum!'

    Phormiōnem, quī Petrōnem bene nōverat, ē vīllā statim ēmīsī.
itaque vīlicus medicum quaerēbat, astrologus mūrem.

---

remedium *cure*

vulnere: vulnus *wound*
effluēbat: effluere
   pour out, flow out
5 **sānāre** *heal, cure*
sciderat: scindere *tear up*
dēligāverat: dēligāre *bind, tie*
lectum: lectus *bed*

10 **numerum: numerus** *number*
arāneārum: arānea
   spider's web
tollēbant: tollere *raise*

15 **collocāvit: collocāre** *place*

prōvīdī: prōvidēre *foresee*
nefāstum: nefāstus *dreadful*
20 **certum: certus**
   certain, infallible
vērī: vērus *true, real*
medicī: medicus *doctor*
mūrem: mūs *mouse*
25 **nigrum: niger** *black*
captum: captus
   captured, caught
dissecāre *cut up*
languidum: languidus *weak,*
30   *feeble*
aurem: auris *ear*

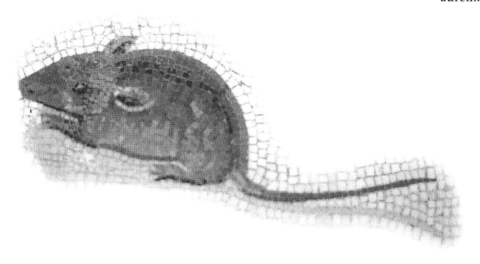

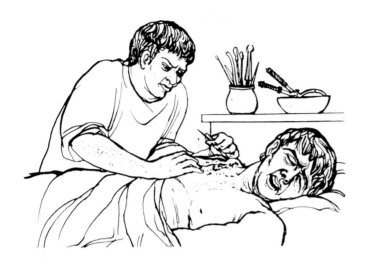

Petrō

Petrō, postquam dē vulnere Barbillī audīvit, statim ad vīllam
eius festīnāvit. ubi cubiculum intrāvit, astrologum vīdit, quī
Barbillum sānāre temptābat. astrologus mūrem dissectum in
vulnus dominī collocābat, versum magicum recitāns. Petrō,
simulac mūrem cōnspexit, īrātissimus erat; astrologum
verberāvit et ē cubiculō expulit.

    tum Petrō, postquam umerum Barbillī īnspexit, spongiam
cēpit et in acētō summersit. eam in vulnus collocāvit. Barbillus
exanimātus reccidit.

    Petrō ad mē sē vertit.

    'necesse est tibi mē adiuvāre', inquit. 'difficile est mihi
Barbillum sānāre. dē vītā eius dēspērō, quod tam multus sanguis
etiam nunc effluit.'

    itaque medicō auxilium dedī. Petrō, postquam aquam
ferventem postulāvit, manūs forcipemque dīligenter lāvit.
deinde, forcipem firmē tenēns, vulnus cum summā cūrā
īnspexit. postquam hoc cōnfēcit, umerum Barbillī lāvit; cutem,
quam hasta servī secuerat, perītē cōnseruit. dēnique umerum
firmē dēligāvit.

    mē ita monuit Petrō:

    'nunc necesse est Barbillō in hōc lectō manēre; necesse est eī
quiēscere et dormīre. nātūra sōla eum sānāre potest, nōn
astrologus.'

    Petrōnī grātiās maximās ēgī. apud Barbillum diū manēbam,
negōtium eius administrāns. Barbillus enim mihi sōlī cōnfīdēbat.
cotīdiē ad cubiculum, ubi iacēbat aeger, veniēbam. multōs
sermōnēs cum Barbillō habēbam, prope lectum sedēns.
postquam Barbillum familiārissimē cognōvī, ille mihi dē vītā suā
multum nārrāvit. sine dubiō fortūna eum graviter afflīxerat.

eius *his*	
dissectum: dissectus *cut up,*	
dismembered	
5	**versum magicum: versus**
	magicus *magic spell*
	spongiam: spongia *sponge*
	acētō: acētum *vinegar*
	summersit: summergere *dip*
10	**reccidit: recidere** *fall back*
15	**ferventem: fervēns** *boiling*
	forcipem: forceps *doctors'*
	tongs, forceps
	firmē *firmly*
	cutem: cutis *skin*
20	**perītē** *skilfully*
	cōnseruit: cōnserere *stitch*
	monuit: monēre *advise*
	quiēscere *rest*
	nātūra *nature*
25	
	familiārissimē: familiāriter
	closely, intimately

About the language 1: present participles

1   Study the following sentences:

> medicus, per forum **ambulāns**, Phormiōnem cōnspexit.
> *The doctor, **walking** through the forum, caught sight of Phormio.*

> Clēmēns Eutychum in mediā viā **stantem** invēnit.
> *Clemens found Eutychus **standing** in the middle of the road.*

> Phormiō ancillās in cubiculō **lacrimantēs** audīvit.
> *Phormio heard the slave-girls **crying** in the bedroom.*

The words in **bold type** are present participles. A present participle is used to describe a noun. For example, in the first sentence, **ambulāns** describes the doctor.

2   Further examples:

   a   astrologus in cubiculum irrūpit, clāmāns.
   b   puerī, per urbem currentēs, Petrōnem cōnspexērunt.
   c   spectātōrēs sacerdōtem ē templō discēdentem vīdērunt.
   d   Galatēa iuvenēs in locō optimō stantēs vituperāvit.

Pick out the present participle in each sentence and find the noun it describes.

3   Study the different forms of the present participle (masculine and feminine):

	SINGULAR			
nominative	portāns	docēns	trahēns	audiēns
accusative	portantem	docentem	trahentem	audientem

	PLURAL			
nominative	portantēs	docentēs	trahentēs	audientēs
accusative	portantēs	docentēs	trahentēs	audientēs

4   Further examples:

   a   fūr ē vīllā effūgit, cachinnāns.
   b   rēx mīlitēs, prō templō sedentēs, spectābat.
   c   Helena in hortō ambulābat, cantāns.
   d   puellae, in pompā ambulantēs, rosās spargēbant.
   e   Clēmēns fēlem sacram in tabernā iacentem invēnit.

Pick out the noun and participle pair in each sentence and state whether it is nominative or accusative, singular or plural.

fortūna crūdēlis

When you have read this story, answer the questions on page 137.

Barbillus uxōrem fidēlem fīliumque optimum habēbat. Plōtīna, uxor Barbillī, erat fēmina placida, quae domī manēbat contenta. Rūfus, fīlius eōrum, erat iuvenis impiger. ad palaestram cum amīcīs saepe adībat; in dēsertīs bēstiās ferōcēs agitāre solēbat. aliquandō, sīcut aliī iuvenēs, contentiōnēs cum parentibus habēbat. sed parentēs Rūfī eum maximē amābant, et ille eōs.

inter amīcōs Rūfī erat iuvenis Athēniēnsis, Eupor. hic Eupor ad urbem Alexandrīam vēnerat et medicīnae studēbat. saepissimē domum Barbillī vīsitābat. tandem ad urbem Athēnās rediit, ubi artem medicīnae exercēbat. Eupor mox epistulam scrīpsit, in quā Rūfum parentēsque ad nūptiās suās invītāvit. Rūfus ad Graeciam īre valdē cupiēbat, sed Barbillus nāvigāre timēbat, quod hiems iam appropinquābat. astrologum suum igitur arcessīvit, et sententiam eius rogāvit. astrologus, postquam diū cōgitāvit, Rūfō parentibusque respōnsum dedit.

'rem perīculōsam suscipitis. lūna Scorpiōnem iam intrat. tūtius est vōbīs domī manēre.'

Barbillus et uxor astrologō, quī erat vir doctissimus, libenter crēdidērunt, sed Rūfus rem graviter ferēbat. ubi Barbillus aberat, Rūfus saepe ad mātrem ībat, patrem dēplōrāns:

'pater stultissimus est, quod astrologō crēdit. astrologī nōn sunt nautae. nihil dē arte nāvigandī sciunt.'

itaque Rūfus Plōtīnae persuāsit, sed patrī persuādēre nōn poterat. Barbillus obstinātus nāvigāre nōluit. Rūfus igitur et Plōtīna Barbillum domī relīquērunt, et ad Graeciam nāvigābant. ubi tamen nāvis, quae eōs vehēbat, Graeciae appropinquābat, ingēns tempestās eam obruit. Rūfus ad lītus natāre poterat, sed Plōtīna, quam Barbillus valdē amābat, in magnīs undīs periit.

ubi Barbillus dē naufragiō, in quō uxor perierat, audīvit, maximē commōtus erat. fīlium iterum vidēre nōlēbat. Rūfus, quamquam domum redīre volēbat, patrī pārēbat. in Graeciā diū manēbat; sed tandem iter in Britanniam fēcit, ubi in exercitū Rōmānō mīlitāvit.

placida: placidus
  calm, peaceful
domī *at home*
eōrum *their*
impiger *lively, energetic*
in dēsertīs *in the desert*
aliquandō *sometimes*
maximē *very much*
Athēniēnsis *Athenian*
medicīnae: medicīna *medicine*
studēbat: studēre *study*
artem: ars *art*
exercēbat: exercēre
  practise, exercise
nūptiās: nūptiae *wedding*
respōnsum *answer*
Scorpiōnem: Scorpiō
  Scorpio (sign of the zodiac)
tūtius est *it would be safer*

nāvigandī *of sailing*

relīquērunt: relinquere *leave*
vehēbat: vehere *carry*
tempestās *storm*
obruit: obruere *overwhelm*

commōtus *upset, distressed*
pārēbat: pārēre *obey*
exercitū: exercitus *army*

5
10
15
20
25
30

Questions

		Marks
1	What are we told about Plotina's character in lines 1–2? Give three details.	3
2	Why is **iuvenis impiger** (line 3) a good description of Rufus? Give two reasons for your answer.	2
3	What kind of a relationship did Rufus have with his parents (lines 5–6)?	2
4	What was Eupor doing in Alexandria?	1
5	When did Eupor write his letter? What did the letter contain (lines 9–11)?	1 + 2
6	Why did Barbillus ask for the opinion of his astrologer (lines 12–14)?	2
7	What was the astrologer's reply (lines 16–17)?	3
8	**Rūfus rem graviter ferēbat**. Why do you think Rufus was upset? What did he do (lines 19–20)?	1 + 2
9	In lines 23–4, did Rufus get all his own way?	2
10	What happened when the ship was approaching Greece? What happened to Rufus and Plotina?	1 + 2
11	Why did Rufus not return home? What did he do after leaving Greece (lines 30–3)?	2 + 2
12	In line 21 Rufus said **'pater stultissimus est, quod astrologō crēdit'**. From what happened to Barbillus and his family, do you think Rufus was right? Give a reason for your answer.	2

TOTAL **30**

Plotina and Rufus would have sailed in a cargo ship like this one. There were no ships that carried only passengers in the Roman world.

About the language 2: eum, eam, etc.

1   You have now met various forms of the Latin word for 'him', 'her', 'them', etc.:

	SINGULAR		PLURAL	
	masculine	*feminine*	*masculine*	*feminine*
accusative	eum	eam	eōs	eās
genitive	eius	eius	eōrum	eārum
dative	eī	eī	eīs	eīs

Clēmēns officīnam intrāvit. Eutychus **eum** salūtāvit.
Clemens entered the workshop. Eutychus greeted him.

servī ingentēs erant. Clēmēns tamen **eōs** neglēxit.
The slaves were huge. However, Clemens ignored them.

Barbillus mē ad cēnam invītāvit. ego ad vīllam **eius** contendī.
Barbillus invited me to dinner. I hurried to his house.

latrōnēs celeriter convēnērunt. Eutychus **eīs** fūstēs trādidit.
The thugs assembled quickly. Eutychus handed out clubs to them.

2   Further examples:

a   Barbillus in cubiculō iacēbat. Quīntus eī vīnum dedit.
b   Galatēa marītum vituperābat. tōta turba eam audīvit.
c   puellae suāviter cantābant. Aristō vōcēs eārum laudāvit.
d   ubi Petrō advēnit, Phormiō eum ad cubiculum dūxit.

astrologus victor

I

astrologus, quī in vīllā Barbillī habitābat, erat vir ingeniī prāvī.
astrologus et Petrō inimīcī erant. astrologus Syrius, medicus
Graecus erat. Petrō artem medicīnae in urbe diū exercuerat.
multī Alexandrīnī, quōs Petrō sānāverat, artem eius laudābant.
    astrologus tamen in vīllā Barbillī habitābat, Petrō in urbe   5
Alexandrīā. facile igitur erat astrologō Barbillum vīsitāre. ad
cubiculum, in quō dominus aeger iacēbat, saepe veniēbat. ubi
Petrō aberat, astrologus in aurem dominī dīcēbat,
    'in perīculō maximō es, domine. Petrō medicus pessimus est.
paucōs sānāvit. multōs aegrōs ad mortem mīsit. num Petrōnī   *10*

vir ingeniī prāvī
    a man of evil character

cōnfīdis? Petrō est vir avārissimus; nēmō est avārior quam ille. pecūniam tuam cupit. necesse est tibi eum ē vīllā expellere.'

Barbillus astrologum anxius audīvit. sed, quamquam dolor cotīdiē ingravēscēbat, medicō etiam nunc crēdēbat. ubi medicum expellere Barbillus nōlēbat, astrologus cōnsilium cēpit. *15*

dolor *pain*	
ingravēscēbat: ingravēscere	
grow worse	

II

postrīdiē astrologus in cubiculum dominī irrūpit, clāmāns:

'domine! tibi nūntium optimum ferō. tē sānāre possum! dea Īsis, quae precēs meās semper audit, noctū somnium ad mē mīsit. in somniō per viās urbis Alexandrīae ambulābam. subitō puerum vīdī in viā stantem. puer erat servus tuus, quem Aegyptiī in tumultū necāvērunt. mihi dē medicāmentō exquīsītissimō nārrāvit.'

Barbillus, ubi hoc audīvit, astrologō sē tōtum trādidit. ille igitur, postquam medicāmentum composuit, umerum dominī aperuit et ūnxit. sed medicāmentum astrologī pessimum erat. ingravēscēbat vulnus Barbillī.

astrologus, ubi hoc sēnsit, ē vīllā fūgit perterritus. Barbillus, dē vītā suā dēspērāns, mē ad cubiculum arcessīvit.

'mī Quīnte', inquit, in aurem susurrāns, 'nōlī lacrimāre! moritūrus sum. id plānē intellegō. necesse est omnibus mortem obīre. hoc ūnum ā tē postulō. fīlium meum in Britanniā quaere! refer eī hanc epistulam! ubi Rūfum ē vīllā expulī īrātus, eī magnam iniūriam intulī. nunc tandem veniam ā Rūfō petō.'

ubi hoc audīvī, Petrōnem arcessere volēbam, sed Barbillus obstinātus recūsābat. arcessīvī tamen illum. sed ubi advēnit, Barbillus iam mortuus erat.

nūntium: nūntius *news*	
precēs *prayers*	
noctū *by night*	
somnium *dream* *5*	
medicāmentō:	
medicāmentum *ointment*	
exquīsītissimō: exquīsītus	
special	
composuit: compōnere *10*	
put together, mix, make up	
ūnxit: unguere *anoint, smear*	
15	
obīre *meet*	
refer: referre *carry, deliver*	
iniūriam intulī: iniūriam	
īnferre *do an injustice to,* *20*	
bring injury to	

A letter from Alexandria, written in Greek on papyrus in the first century AD.

Practising the language

1 Complete each sentence with the right form of the participle. Then translate the sentence.

    a   Barbillus, dē vītā ...., Quīntum arcessīvit.
        (dēspērāns, dēspērantēs)

    b   Quīntus lībertum in tabernā .... invēnit.
        (labōrāns, labōrantem)

    c   sacerdōtēs, prō templō ...., silentium poposcērunt.
        (stāns, stantēs)

    d   hippopotamum .... nōn cōnspexī.
        (adveniēns, advenientem)

    e   Aegyptiī per viās cucurrērunt, magnum clāmōrem ....
        .(tollēns, tollentēs)

    f   Clēmēns tabernāriōs ā latrōnibus .... vīdit.
        (fugiēns, fugientēs)

    g   puer mortuus dēcidit, dominum ....
        (dēfendēns, dēfendentem, dēfendentēs)

    h   Aristō iuvenēs versum scurrīlem .... audīvit.
        (recitāns, recitantem, recitantēs)

2 Complete each sentence with the right form of the verb. Then translate the sentence.

    a   Barbillus: Quīnte! mēcum ad vēnātiōnem ....!
                   (venī, venīte)

    b   Phormiō: servī! ad flūmen Nīlum ....!
                   (prōcēde, prōcēdite)

    c   astrologus: domine! .... ē vīllā discēdere! (nōlī, nōlīte)

    d   Quīntus: amīce! nōlī astrologō ....! (crēde, crēdere)

    e   Phormiō: servī! ad mediam palūdem cautē ....!
                   (nāvigā, nāvigāte)

    f   Barbillus: Aethiopes! hastās ....! (ēmitte, ēmittite)

    g   Quīntus: servī! .... hippopotamum vexāre!
                   (nōlī, nōlīte)

    h   Barbillus: Quīnte! vulnerātus sum. mē ....!
                   (servā, servāte)

3 Translate into English:

Narcissus

Aristō: Galatēa! fortūna nōbīs favet! iuvenis Narcissus, quem herī vīdimus, Helenae dōnum mīsit. dōnum quod iuvenis mīsit, pretiōsissimum est. dōnum mihi quoque mīsit. iuvenis Narcissus Helenam nostram amat.   *5*

Galatēa: quid dīcis, asine? iuvenis, quī prope nōs stābat, fīliae nostrae dōnum mīsit? ēheu! marītum stultissimum habeō. parentēs Narcissī humilēs sunt. māter est Aegyptia, pater caupō. taberna, quam tenet, sordida est.   *10*

humilēs: humilis *low-born, of low class*

Aristō: parentēs, quōs vituperās, nōn nōvī. sed Narcissus ipse probus et benignus est. iuvenis etiam līberālis est. libellum enim mihi dedit. (*Aristō libellum īnspicit.*) ēheu! Narcissus poēta est. suōs versūs scurrīlēs mihi mīsit.   *15*

libellum: libellus *little book*

Galatēa: fortūna nōbīs favet! nunc marītus meus illī iuvenī Helenam dare nōn vult.

Write out the relative clauses in this story and state the noun which each relative clause describes.

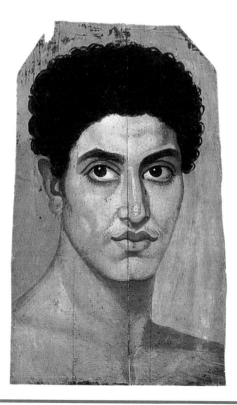

Narcissus.

Medicine and science

Soon after its foundation, Alexandria became famous as a centre of science and learning. The Museum and its Library, which were set up and financed by the Greek rulers of Egypt, attracted clever men from all over the Greek world, who quickly began to make discoveries in all the sciences, including medicine. A good beginning had already been made in medicine by the Greek, Hippocrates, who had attempted to remove magic and superstition from the treatment of disease by observing his patients' symptoms carefully and trying to discover their causes. Hippocrates, who lived on the island of Cos in the fifth century BC, was rightly regarded as the founder of medical science. He and his followers pledged themselves to high standards of conduct in the famous Hippocratic oath. Part of it reads as follows:

A seal stone carved with a picture of a doctor examining a patient, supervised by Aesculapius, the god of healing.

> *'Into whatever houses I enter, I will go into them for the benefit of the sick, and will abstain from every voluntary act of mischief and corruption. Whatever in my professional practice I see or hear, which ought not to be spoken abroad, I will not divulge.'*

But Hippocrates and his Greek followers usually investigated only the surface of the body and not its interior; this was because the Greeks felt the idea of dissecting a body was disagreeable and perhaps wicked. The Egyptians, however, with their ancient custom of mummifying corpses, had a different attitude to the body, and dissections of corpses may have been performed by Egyptian doctors. Alexandria was therefore a good place for studying anatomy. Herophilus, the most famous Alexandrian

Alexandrian doctors were particularly expert about the inside of the body, although others had some knowledge. This clay model of the intestines, and models of other body parts, were dedicated to the gods by patients at a healing shrine in Italy.

anatomist, gave a detailed description of the brain, explained the differences between tendons and nerves, arteries and veins, and described the optic nerve and the eye, including the retina. He also measured the frequency of the pulse and used this to diagnose fever. Like earlier doctors, he laid great stress on the importance of hygiene, diet, exercise and bathing.

In addition to general advice of this kind, an experienced doctor of the first century AD would treat minor ailments with drugs. The juice of the wild poppy, which contains opium, was used to relieve pain. Unwashed sheep's wool, containing lanolin, was often applied to wounds and swellings to soothe the irritation. Many prescriptions, however, would have been useless. For example, one account of the treatment of chilblains begins: 'In the first place the chilblains are to be fomented thoroughly with boiled turnips…'. Any benefit felt by the patient would be due not to the turnips, but to the heat of the fomentation or the patient's own belief that the treatment would do him good.

Some prescriptions are rather alarming, such as this for severe toothache: 'When a tooth decays, there is no great need to remove it, but if the pain compels its removal, a peppercorn or an ivy berry should be inserted into the cavity of the tooth, which will then split and fall out in bits.'

Minor surgery was regularly practised: 'Tonsils are covered by a thin layer of skin. If they become hardened after inflammation, they should be scratched round with a finger and drawn out. If they cannot be drawn out in this way they should be gripped with a hook and cut out with a scalpel. The hollow should then be swilled out with vinegar and the wound smeared with something to check the blood.'

Fractures and wounds presented greater problems. Nevertheless, doctors were able to make incisions, tie veins and arteries, reset broken bones with splints, and stitch up wounds. Difficult or very delicate operations were sometimes attempted, such as operations on the eye to relieve cataracts. Amputation of limbs was undertaken as a last resort.

Like Petro in the story on page 134, Greek doctors insisted on high standards of cleanliness in operations, to reduce the risk of infection. Although the quality of medical treatment in the ancient world would naturally vary considerably from one doctor to another, it is probably true that the standards of the best doctors were not improved upon in western Europe until about a hundred and fifty years ago.

The Museum at Alexandria was also famous for the study of mathematics. Euclid, who worked there in the third century BC, wrote a book known as the *Elements*, in which he summarised all previous knowledge of geometry; it continued to be used as a school textbook until relatively recent times. In applying their mathematical knowledge to the world around them, the Greeks

A set of medical instruments carved on the walls of an Egyptian temple about 25 years after Quintus' visit to Alexandria. In the third row notice the scales for weighing medicines, and the forceps. The cups in the bottom left corner were used to draw off blood.

The bronze cup was heated and its mouth was applied to a patch of skin whose surface had been cut or scratched. As the air in the cup cooled, blood was gently sucked out.

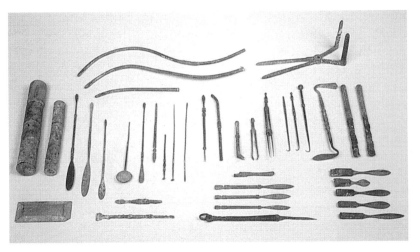

A Roman doctor had a wide range of instruments at his disposal.

A saw for cutting through bone.

A stamp for labelling cakes of eye ointment and a plaster cast of the impressions of the four sides.

at Alexandria reached some very accurate conclusions. For example, Eratosthenes calculated that the circumference of the Earth was 24,662 miles (39,459 km); this is remarkably close to the true figure of 24,860 miles (40,008 km).

Astronomy, which had begun in Babylon, developed further at Alexandria. Astronomers at Alexandria made the first attempts at calculating the distances between the Earth and the Sun and between the Earth and the Moon. The idea was also put forward that the Earth was round, rotated on its axis and circled the Sun with the other planets. After the end of the western Roman Empire in the fifth century AD, this idea was forgotten until Copernicus rediscovered it in the sixteenth century. It is remarkable that Alexandrian astronomers devised their theories

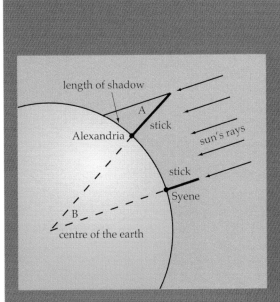

Diagram of Eratosthenes' experiment

*Eratosthenes discovered that at Syene (modern Aswan) in southern Egypt the sun was directly overhead at noon on the day of the summer solstice so that a vertical stick cast no shadow. At the same moment, the sun in Alexandria (which Eratosthenes believed was due north of Syene) was **not** directly overhead, so that a stick in Alexandria **did** cast a shadow. Eratosthenes measured this shadow and used his measurement to calculate the angle A between the sun's rays and the stick. Since the sun's rays are parallel, angle B is the same as angle A. Knowing angle B and the distance between Syene and Alexandria, he was able to calculate the circumference of the Earth.*

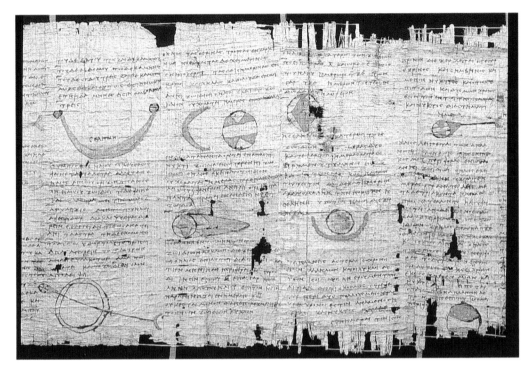

Part of a papyrus treatise on astronomy, written in Greek at Alexandria in the 2nd century BC.

and made their calculations without the aid of telescopes or other accurate instruments.

Hero of Alexandria invented the first steam turbine, in the form of a toy, in which a hollow ball was mounted on two brackets on the lid of a vessel of boiling water. One bracket was hollow and conducted steam from the vessel into the ball. The steam escaped from the ball by means of two bent pipes, thus creating a force which made the ball spin round. He also made a hollow altar, where, when a fire was lit, hot air streamed through four bent pipes to make puppets dance.

However, the Alexandrians did not take advantage of their scientific discoveries to build complicated and powerful machines for use in industry. Perhaps they felt they had no need for such machines, as they had a large work-force of slaves and free men; perhaps they regarded trade and manufacturing as less dignified than scientific research and investigation; or perhaps they were prevented from developing industrial machinery by their lack of technical skills such as the ability to make large metal containers and hold them together by screws and welds. Whatever the reason, some of the discoveries made by the Alexandrians were not put to practical use until many centuries later.

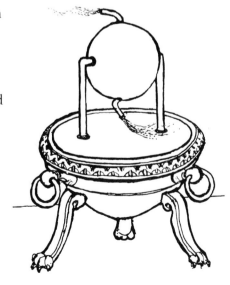

Hero's steam turbine.

Vocabulary checklist 20

adeō, adīre, adiī	go up to, approach
arcessō, arcessere, arcessīvī	summon, send for
ars, artis	art
crūdēlis	cruel
dēnique	at last, finally
dēspērō, dēspērāre, dēspērāvī	despair
doctus, docta, doctum	learned, clever
domus, domūs	home
īnferō, īnferre, intulī	bring in, bring on
līberō, līberāre, līberāvī	free, set free
lūna, lūnae	moon
mors, mortis	death
oculus, oculī	eye
persuādeō, persuādēre, persuāsī	persuade
pessimus, pessima, pessimum	very bad, worst
relinquō, relinquere, relīquī	leave
sīcut	like
tam	so
temptō, temptāre, temptāvī	try
vulnus, vulneris	wound

ūnus	one
duo	two
trēs	three
quattuor	four
quīnque	five
sex	six
septem	seven
octō	eight
novem	nine
decem	ten
vīgintī	twenty
trīgintā	thirty
quadrāgintā	forty
quīnquāgintā	fifty

LANGUAGE INFORMATION

Contents

Part One: About the language

Nouns

	first declension	second declension		
gender	f.	m.	m.	n.
SINGULAR				
nominative and vocative	puella	servus (*voc.* serve)	puer	templum
accusative	puellam	servum	puerum	templum
genitive (of)	puellae	servī	puerī	templī
dative (to, for)	puellae	servō	puerō	templō
PLURAL				
nominative and vocative	puellae	servī	puerī	
accusative	puellās	servōs	puerōs	
genitive (of)	puellārum	servōrum	puerōrum	
dative (to, for)	puellīs	servīs	puerīs	

Notes:

1   The vocative case is used when someone is being spoken to:
     ubi es, serve?   *Where are you, slave?*

2   Some 2nd declension nouns such as **puer** have a nominative and vocative singular ending in **-er**. All their other cases are formed like the cases of **servus**.

3   1st declension nouns like **puella** are usually feminine.
    2nd declension nouns are usually either masculine like **servus**, or neuter like **templum**.
    3rd declension nouns may be either masculine like **mercātor**, or feminine like **urbs**, or neuter like **nōmen**.

4   Study the two nouns **templum** and **nōmen**. Notice that the forms **templum** and **nōmen** can be either nominative or accusative. This is because **templum** and **nōmen** are *neuter*. Every neuter noun uses the same form for both its nominative and accusative singular. (You have not yet met the nominative and accusative plural of neuter nouns.)

third declension

m.	m.	m.	m.	f.	n.	*gender*
						SINGULAR
mercātor	leō	cīvis	rēx	urbs	nōmen	*nominative and vocative*
mercātōrem	leōnem	cīvem	rēgem	urbem	nōmen	*accusative*
mercātōris	leōnis	cīvis	rēgis	urbis	nōminis	*genitive (of)*
mercātōrī	leōnī	cīvī	rēgī	urbī	nōminī	*dative (to, for)*
						PLURAL
mercātōrēs	leōnēs	cīvēs	rēgēs	urbēs		*nominative and vocative*
mercātōrēs	leōnēs	cīvēs	rēgēs	urbēs		*accusative*
mercātōrum	leōnum	cīvium	rēgum	urbium		*genitive (of)*
mercātōribus	leōnibus	cīvibus	rēgibus	urbibus		*dative (to, for)*

5   With the help of the noun tables find the Latin for the words in **bold type** in the following sentences.

    a   We saw the **lion** in the wood.
    b   The **slave-girls** were working in the bedroom.
    c   Salvius and Quintus gave their presents to the **king**.
    d   Many **merchants** travelled to Britain.
    e   The master gave a reward to his brave **slaves**.
    f   The eruption terrified the **citizens**.
    g   The **boy** did not believe his father.
    h   Do you like this **city**?

6   Translate the following sentences, which contain examples of the dative case.

    a   Vārica dominō pecūniam trādidit.
    b   rēx uxōrī dōnum compārāvit.
    c   imperātor lībertīs et cīvibus spectāculum dedit.
    d   Salvius vīlicō et agricolae canem ostendit.
    e   puer iuvenibus et senī rem nārrāvit.
    f   ancillae mercātōrī et mīlitibus triclīnium parāvērunt.
    g   coquus dominō et amīcīs respondit.
    h   nūntius cīvī et nautae crēdēbat.

7   The **genitive case** is introduced in Stage 17.

> puer ad tabernam **Clēmentis** cucurrit.
> *The boy ran to **Clemens'** shop.*

> spectātōrēs clāmābant, sed rēx clāmōrēs **spectātōrum** nōn audīvit.
> *The spectators were shouting, but the king did not hear the shouts **of the spectators**.*

> iuvenis vōcem **fēminae** laudāvit.
> *The young man praised the **woman's** voice.*

Further examples:

a   Quīntus, quī prope nāvem stābat, vōcēs nautārum audīvit.
b   Īsis erat dea Aegyptia. sacerdōtēs ad templum deae cotīdiē ībant.
c   magna multitūdō mīlitum in viā nōbīs obstābat.
d   clāmōrēs puerōrum senem vexābant.
e   prīncipēs ad aulam rēgis quam celerrimē contendērunt.
f   in vīllā amīcī meī saepe cēnābam.

8   The following sentences include examples of the cases in the noun tables
on pages 150–1. Translate the sentences and then write down the case and number of
the nouns in bold type.

a   mercātōrēs Alexandrīnī **nāvēs** spectābant.
b   Clēmēns dōnum pretiōsum **deae** obtulit.
c   **tabernāriī**, latrōnibus resistite!
d   domina stolās novās **ancillīs** dedit.
e   hasta caput **mīlitis** percussit.
f   puerum necāvērunt **Aegyptiī**.
g   Augustus illud **templum** aedificāvit.
h   vōcēs **prīncipum** in aulā audīvimus.

Adjectives

1   In Stages 14 and 18 you have seen how an adjective changes its endings to agree with the noun it describes in three ways: case, number and gender.

2   Most adjectives in Latin belong either to the 1st and 2nd declension or to the 3rd declension. The adjective **bonus** 'good' belongs to the 1st and 2nd declension:

		SINGULAR		PLURAL	
	masculine	*feminine*	*neuter*	*masculine*	*feminine*
nominative and vocative	bonus (*voc.* bone)	bona	bonum	bonī	bonae
accusative	bonum	bonam	bonum	bonōs	bonās
genitive	bonī	bonae	bonī	bonōrum	bonārum
dative	bonō	bonae	bonō	bonīs	bonīs

Compare the endings of **bonus** with those of the 1st and 2nd declension nouns **servus**, **puella** and **templum** listed on page 150.

3   The adjective **fortis** 'brave' belongs to the 3rd declension:

	SINGULAR	PLURAL
	masculine and feminine	*masculine and feminine*
nominative and vocative	fortis	fortēs
accusative	fortem	fortēs
genitive	fortis	fortium
dative	fortī	fortibus

Compare the endings of **fortis** with those of the 3rd declension noun **cīvis** listed on page 151.

4   With the help of paragraphs 2 and 3, find the Latin words for 'good' and 'brave' in each of the following sentences.

a   The merchant praised his good daughter.
b   The king greeted the brave soldiers.
c   The good men were working hard.
d   A brave woman resisted the enemy.
e   The master gave a reward to the brave boys.
f   The craftsmen made a statue of the good emperor.
g   The leader of the brave citizens was wounded.
h   The father left money to his good wife.

Comparatives and superlatives

1 In Stage 8, you met the **superlative** form of the adjective:

> Clēmēns est **laetissimus**.   coquus est **stultissimus**.
> *Clemens is **very happy**.*   *The cook is **very stupid**.*

2 In Stage 10, you met the **comparative** form:

> gladiātor erat **fortior** quam leō.   estis **stultiōrēs** quam asinī!
> *The gladiator was **braver** than a lion.*   *You are **more stupid** than donkeys!*

3 Study the way in which the comparative and superlative are formed:

nominative	accusative	comparative (more...)	superlative (very...)
longus *long*	longum	longior *longer*	longissimus *very long*
pulcher *beautiful*	pulchrum	pulchrior *more beautiful*	pulcherrimus *very beautiful*
fortis *brave*	fortem	fortior *braver*	fortissimus *very brave*
ferōx *fierce*	ferōcem	ferōcior *more fierce*	ferōcissimus *very fierce*

4 The comparative and superlative forms change their endings in the usual way to indicate case, number and gender:

nominative	leō **saevissimus** intrāvit. *A **very fierce** lion entered.*
accusative	leōnem **saevissimum** interfēcī. *I killed a **very fierce** lion.*
singular	Dumnorix est **callidior** quam Belimicus. *Dumnorix is **cleverer** than Belimicus.*
plural	Rēgnēnsēs sunt **callidiōrēs** quam Canticī. *The Regnenses are **cleverer** than the Cantici.*
masculine	dominus meus est **īrātissimus**. *My master is **very angry**.*
feminine	uxor mea est **īrātissima**. *My wife is **very angry**.*

5 Some important adjectives form their comparatives and superlatives in an irregular way:

bonus	melior	optimus
good	*better*	*very good, best*
magnus	maior	maximus
big	*bigger*	*very big*

and

multus	plūs	plūrimus
much	*more*	*very much*

which becomes in the plural:

multī	plūrēs	plūrimī
many	*more*	*very many*

6 Further examples:

a leō erat maior quam Herculēs.
b Clēmēns plūrēs amīcōs quam Eutychus habēbat.
c Aristō erat poēta melior quam Barbillus.
d Quīntus numquam nāvēs maiōrēs vīderat.

7 Translate each sentence, then change the adjective in **bold type** into the superlative form, and translate again.

For example: ātrium **magnum** erat.   This becomes: ātrium **maximum** erat.
          The hall was **big**.   *The hall was* **very big**.

a vīlicus puerōs **bonōs** laudāvit.
b **multī** cīvēs in flammīs periērunt.
c Quīntus servīs **bonīs** lībertātem dedit.
d Herculēs erat **magnus**, et **magnum** fūstem habēbat.

8 Translate the first sentence of each pair. Complete the second sentence with the comparative and superlative of the adjective given in brackets at the end of the sentence. Use the first sentence as a guide. Then translate the second sentence.

a canis est **stultissimus**; canem **stultiōrem** numquam vīdī. (stultus)
  Volūbilis est . . . .; servum . . . . numquam vīdī. (laetus)

b frāter meus est sapientior quam tū; sapientissimus est. (sapiēns)
  Bregāns est . . . . quam Loquāx; . . . . est. (īnsolēns)

c mīlitēs sunt fortiōrēs quam cīvēs; fortissimī sunt. (fortis)
  servī sunt . . . . quam lībertī; . . . . sunt. (trīstis)

d Melissa vōcem suāvissimam habēbat; vōcem suāviōrem numquam audīvī. (suāvis)
  Caecilius servum . . . . habēbat; servum . . . . numquam vīdī. (fidēlis)

Pronouns I: ego, tū, nōs, vōs, sē

1   In Book I, you met the Latin words for 'I', 'you' (singular), 'me', etc.:

nominative	ego	tū
accusative	mē	tē
dative	mihi	tibi

domina **tē** laudāvit.
*The mistress praised **you**.*

senex **mihi** illum equum dedit.
*The old man gave that horse **to me**.*

2   You also met the words for 'we', 'you' (plural), 'us', etc.:

nominative	nōs	vōs
accusative	nōs	vōs
dative	nōbīs	vōbīs

nōs Rōmānī sumus mīlitēs.
***We** Romans are soldiers.*

dominus **vōs** īnspicere vult.
*The master wants to inspect **you**.*

3   Note the Latin for 'with me', 'with you', etc.:

Salvius **mēcum** ambulābat.
*Salvius was walking **with me**.*

Rūfilla **tēcum** sedēbat.
*Rufilla was sitting **with you**.*

rēx **nōbīscum** cēnābat.
*The king was dining **with us**.*

iuvenēs **vōbīscum** pugnābant?
*Were the young men fighting **with you**?*

Compare this with the usual Latin way of saying 'with':

rēx **cum Salviō** ambulābat.
*The king was walking **with Salvius**.*

mīlitēs **cum iuvenibus** pugnābant.
*The soldiers were fighting **with the young men**.*

4   Further examples:

a   ego tibi pecūniam dedī.
b   rēx nōs ad aulam invītāvit.
c   Cogidubnus nōbīscum sedēbat.
d   cūr mē vituperās?
e   nōs ancillae semper labōrāmus.
f   necesse est vōbīs mēcum venīre.
g   vōs Quīntō crēditis, sed Salvius mihi crēdit.
h   tē pūnīre possum, quod ego sum dominus.

5 The words **ego**, **tū**, etc. belong to a group of words known as pronouns. Pronouns are used in sentences in a very similar way to nouns. For example, this sentence uses the noun 'Salvius':

> Salvius est dominus.   *Salvius is the master.*

But if Salvius himself were the speaker of the sentence, he would not use the noun 'Salvius' but the pronoun **ego**:

> **ego** sum dominus.   **I** *am the master.*

And somebody speaking to Salvius would replace the noun 'Salvius' with the pronoun **tū**:

> **tū** es dominus   **You** *are the master.*

6 You have also met the pronoun **sē**, meaning 'himself', 'herself' or 'themselves'. It has the same form for both singular and plural, and it has no nominative case:

	SINGULAR	PLURAL
accusative	sē	sē
dative	sibi	sibi

Dumnorix in ursam **sē** coniēcit.
*Dumnorix hurled **himself** at the bear.*

rēgīna **sē** interfēcit.
*The queen killed **herself**.*

servī in ōrdinēs longōs **sē** īnstrūxērunt.
*The slaves drew **themselves** up in long lines.*

mercātor **sibi** vīllam ēmit.
*The merchant bought the house **for himself**.*

Pronouns II: **hic, ille, eum**

1   In Stage 19, you met the following forms of the word **hic** meaning 'this' (plural 'these'):

	SINGULAR			PLURAL	
	masculine	*feminine*	*neuter*	*masculine*	*feminine*
nominative	hic	haec	hoc	hī	hae
accusative	hunc	hanc	hoc	hōs	hās

hae stolae sunt sordidae!
These dresses are dirty!

hunc servum pūnīre volō.
*I want to punish **this** slave.*

2   You have also met the following forms of the word **ille** meaning 'that' (plural 'those'):

	SINGULAR			PLURAL	
	masculine	*feminine*	*neuter*	*masculine*	*feminine*
nominative	ille	illa	illud	illī	illae
accusative	illum	illam	illud	illōs	illās

illa taberna nunc est mea.
That shop is now mine.

spectā **illōs** hominēs!
*Look at **those** men!*

3   In Stage 20, the following forms of the word for 'him', 'her' and 'them' were listed:

	SINGULAR		PLURAL	
	masculine	*feminine*	*masculine*	*feminine*
accusative	eum	eam	eōs	eās
genitive	eius	eius	eōrum	eārum
dative	eī	eī	eīs	eīs

iuvenēs **eam** laudāvērunt.
*The young men praised **her**.*

ego ad vīllam **eius** contendī.
*I hurried to **his** house.*

dominus **eī** praemium dedit.
*The master gave a reward **to him**.*

senex **eīs** crēdere nōluit.
*The old man was unwilling to trust **them**.*

4   The various forms of the word **ille** can also be used to mean 'he', 'him' (masculine), 'she', 'her' (feminine), 'they', 'them' (plural):

ille tamen nōn erat perterritus.
***He**, however, was not terrified.*

nēmō **illam** in urbe vīdit.
*No one saw **her** in the city.*

Pronouns III: quī

1   In Stages 15 and 16, you met various forms of the **relative pronoun quī**, which is placed at the start of a relative clause and means 'who', 'which', etc.:

	SINGULAR			PLURAL	
	masculine	*feminine*	*neuter*	*masculine*	*feminine*
nominative	quī	quae	quod	quī	quae
accusative	quem	quam	quod	quōs	quās

ursa, **quam** Quīntus vulnerāvit, nunc mortua est.
*The bear **which** Quintus wounded is now dead.*

ubi est templum, **quod** Augustus Caesar aedificāvit?
*Where is the temple **which** Augustus Caesar built?*

in mediō ātriō stābant mīlitēs, **quī** rēgem custōdiēbant.
*In the middle of the hall stood the soldiers, **who** were guarding the king.*

The noun described by a relative clause is known as the antecedent of the relative pronoun. For example, in the first Latin sentence above, **ursa** is the antecedent of **quam**.

2   Translate the following sentences.

    a   flōrēs, quī in hortō erant, rēgem delectāvērunt.
    b   puer, quem Aegyptiī interfēcērunt, Quīntum fortiter dēfendēbat.
    c   fabrī, quōs rēx ex Ītaliā arcessīverat, effigiem Claudiī fēcērunt.
    d   cubiculum, quod Quīntus intrāvit, ēlegantissimum erat.

In each sentence pick out the antecedent and the relative pronoun.

3   The following sentences include the different pronouns described on pages 156–9.

    a   postquam senex hoc dīxit, Barbillus eum laudāvit.
    b   in palaestrā erant multī āthlētae, quī sē exercēbant.
    c   quamquam puellae prope mē stābant, eās vidēre nōn poteram.
    d   illud est vīnum, quod Cogidubnus ex Ītaliā importāvit.
    e   simulac mercātōrēs advēnērunt, Clēmēns eīs pecūniam trādidit.
    f   dā mihi illum fūstem!
    g   mīlitēs, quōs imperātor mīserat, nōbīscum sedēbant.
    h   Barbillus hās statuās sibi ēmit.
    i   rēgīna, quae tē honōrāvit, nōs vituperāvit.
    j   simulac latrō hanc tabernam intrāvit, vōcem eius audīvī.

Verbs

	first conjugation	second conjugation	third conjugation	fourth conjugation
PRESENT TENSE	*I carry, you carry, etc.*	*I teach, you teach, etc.*	*I drag, you drag, etc.*	*I hear, you hear, etc.*
	portō	doceō	trahō	audiō
	portās	docēs	trahis	audīs
	portat	docet	trahit	audit
	portāmus	docēmus	trahimus	audīmus
	portātis	docētis	trahitis	audītis
	portant	docent	trahunt	audiunt
IMPERFECT TENSE	*I was carrying*	*I was teaching*	*I was dragging*	*I was hearing*
	portābam	docēbam	trahēbam	audiēbam
	portābās	docēbās	trahēbās	audiēbās
	portābat	docēbat	trahēbat	audiēbat
	portābāmus	docēbāmus	trahēbāmus	audiēbāmus
	portābātis	docēbātis	trahēbātis	audiēbātis
	portābant	docēbant	trahēbant	audiēbant
PERFECT TENSE	*I (have) carried*	*I (have) taught*	*I (have) dragged*	*I (have) heard*
	portāvī	docuī	trāxī	audīvī
	portāvistī	docuistī	trāxistī	audīvistī
	portāvit	docuit	trāxit	audīvit
	portāvimus	docuimus	trāximus	audīvimus
	portāvistis	docuistis	trāxistis	audīvistis
	portāvērunt	docuērunt	trāxērunt	audīvērunt
PLUPERFECT TENSE	*I had carried*	*I had taught*	*I had dragged*	*I had heard*
	portāveram	docueram	trāxeram	audīveram
	portāverās	docuerās	trāxerās	audīverās
	portāverat	docuerat	trāxerat	audīverat
	portāverāmus	docuerāmus	trāxerāmus	audīverāmus
	portāverātis	docuerātis	trāxerātis	audīverātis
	portāverant	docuerant	trāxerant	audīverant
INFINITIVE	*to carry*	*to teach*	*to drag*	*to hear*
	portāre	docēre	trahere	audīre
IMPERATIVE	*carry!*	*teach!*	*drag!*	*hear!*
	portā	docē	trahe	audī
	portāte	docēte	trahite	audīte

1   Translate the following examples:

portābant; portāvimus; trahēbās; trahitis;
docuērunt; audīvī; portābāmus; docuistī

2   Translate the following examples, then change them to mean 'I ...' instead of 'he ...' and
translate again.

trahēbat; audīvit; docet;
intrāvit; dormiēbat; sedet

3   Translate the following examples, then change them from the plural to the singular,
so that they mean 'you (singular) ...' instead of 'they...', and translate again.

portāvērunt; trahunt; audīverant; manēbant; laudant; intellēxērunt

Persons and endings

1   The forms of the verb which indicate 'I', 'you' (singular) and 'he' (or 'she'
or 'it') are known as 1st, 2nd and 3rd person singular.
The forms which indicate 'we', 'you' (plural) and 'they' are known as the
1st, 2nd and 3rd person plural.

The following table summarises the Latin verb endings and the English
translations which are used to indicate the different persons:

English		Latin verb ending	
		PRESENT	
		IMPERFECT	
		PLUPERFECT	PERFECT
I	1st person singular	-ō or -m	-ī
you	2nd person singular	-s	-istī
he, she, it	3rd person singular	-t	-it
we	1st person plural	-mus	-imus
you	2nd person plural	-tis	-istis
they	3rd person plural	-nt	-ērunt

So a word like **trāxerant** can be either translated (*they had dragged*) or
described (3rd person plural pluperfect). Two further examples, **portāvī** and **docent**,
are translated and described as follows:

portāvī   *I carried*   1st person singular perfect
docent   *they teach*   3rd person plural present

2   Describe and translate the following examples.

trāxī; audīs; portābāmus; docuerant; ambulāvistī; dīxerat

Irregular verbs

PRESENT TENSE	*I am*	*I am able*	*I want*	*I bring*
	sum	possum	volō	ferō
	es	potes	vīs	fers
	est	potest	vult	fert
	sumus	possumus	volumus	ferimus
	estis	potestis	vultis	fertis
	sunt	possunt	volunt	ferunt
PERFECT TENSE		*I have been able*	*I (have) wanted*	*I (have) brought*
IMPERFECT TENSE	*I was*	*I was able*	*I was wanting*	*I was bringing*
	eram	poteram	volēbam	ferēbam
	erās	poterās	volēbās	ferēbās
	erat	poterat	volēbat	ferēbat
	erāmus	poterāmus	volēbāmus	ferēbāmus
	erātis	poterātis	volēbātis	ferēbātis
	erant	poterant	volēbant	ferēbant
PERFECT TENSE		*I have been able*	*I (have) wanted*	*I (have) brought*
		potuī	voluī	tulī
		potuistī	voluistī	tulistī
		potuit	voluit	tulit
		potuimus	voluimus	tulimus
		potuistis	voluistis	tulistis
		potuērunt	voluērunt	tulērunt
PLUPERFECT TENSE		*I had been able*	*I had wanted*	*I had brought*
		potueram	volueram	tuleram
		potuerās	voluerās	tulerās
		potuerat	voluerat	tulerat
		potuerāmus	voluerāmus	tulerāmus
		potuerātis	voluerātis	tulerātis
		potuerant	voluerant	tulerant
INFINITIVE	*to be*	*to be able*	*to want*	*to bring*
	esse	posse	velle	ferre

1   Notice the difference between the present and perfect tenses of **ferō**:

      ferō   *I bring*   tulī   *I brought*

Compare this with the way the word 'go' changes in English:

      I go, you go, etc.   *I went, you went, etc.*

2   The verbs **absum** (*I am absent*) and **adsum** (*I am present*) are formed by
adding **ab** and **ad** to the forms of **sum**. For example:

est	*he is*	adest	*he is present*	abest	*he is absent*
erat	*he was*	aderat	*he was present*	aberat	*he was absent*

3   Translate the following examples.

es	ades	ferunt
poterāmus	aberant	voluistī
tulit	sumus	ferēbātis
vīs	aderātis	abesse

Verbs with the dative

1   In Book I, you met a number of verbs, such as **faveō** and **crēdō**, which are often used with a noun in the dative case. For example:

    mercātōrēs **Holcōniō** favēbant.
    *The merchants gave their support **to Holconius**.*
or *The merchants supported Holconius.*

2   You have now met some other verbs which are used in the same way:

    turba **nōbīs** obstat.
    *The crowd is an obstacle **to us**.*
or *The crowd is obstructing us.*

    Clēmēns **latrōnibus** resistēbat.
    *Clemens put up a resistance **to the thugs**.*
or *Clemens resisted the thugs.*

3   Further examples:

a   Barbillus Quīntō cōnfīdēbat.
b   mīlitibus resistere nōn potuimus.
c   tandem fīlius mātrī persuāsit.
d   sacerdōtēs lentē templō appropinquāvērunt.

Word order

The word order in the following sentences is very common:

1 clāmābant Rēgnēnsēs.   intrāvit Cogidubnus.
The Regnenses were shouting.   *Cogidubnus entered.*

Further examples:

   a   lacrimābant ancillae.   **c**   dormiēbat rēx.
   b   labōrābat Clēmēns.   **d**   rīdēbant puerī.

2 amīcum salūtāvit.   ancillās laudāvimus.
He greeted his friend.   *We praised the slave-girls.*

Further examples:

   a   cēnam parābant.   **c**   pecūniam invēnit.
   b   dominōs audīvimus.   **d**   mātrem vīdistis?

The following word orders are also found:

3 discum petēbat āthlēta.   nautās vituperābat Belimicus.
The athlete was looking for the discus.   *Belimicus was cursing the sailors.*

Further examples:

   a   amphoram portābat vīlicus.   **c**   gladiātōrēs laudāvit nūntius.
   b   vīnum bibēbant prīncipēs.   **d**   rosās spargēbant puellae.

4 mercātōrem rēx dēcēpit.   equum agricola vēndidit.
The king deceived the merchant.   *The farmer sold the horse.*

Further examples:

   a   fēminās dominus spectābat.   **c**   poētās rēgīna honōrāvit.
   b   leōnem gladiātor interfēcit.   **d**   templum sacerdōs intrāvit.

5 The following sentences include all the different sorts of word order used in paragraphs 1–4:

   a   surrēxērunt prīncipēs.   **d**   rēgem cīvēs vīdērunt.
   b   togam gerēbat.   **e**   mē dēcēpistī.
   c   multitūdinem incitābat senex. **f**   fīlium pater vituperābat.

6 The following examples each contain a noun in the dative case:

nūntiō epistulam dedī.
I gave a letter to the messenger.

amīcīs crēdēbat.
He believed his friends.

Further examples:

a mercātōrī pecūniam reddidit.
b mīlitibus cibum parāvī.

c dominō resistēbant.
d tibi faveō.

Longer sentences I: with **postquam, simulac**, etc.

1   In Book I you met sentences like this:

>   Salvius, postquam fundum īnspexit, ad vīllam revēnit.
>   *Salvius, after he inspected the farm, returned to the house.*

Or, in more natural English:
After Salvius inspected the farm, he returned to the house.

2   You also met sentences which are like the one above but also contain a noun in the dative case. For example:

>   Rūfilla, postquam Salviō rem nārrāvit, exiit.
>   *Rufilla, after she told the story to Salvius, went out.*

Or, in more natural English:
After Rufilla told Salvius the story, she went out.

3   Further examples:

   a   geminī, postquam coquō cibum trādidērunt, ē culīnā discessērunt.
   b   nūntius, postquam cīvibus spectāculum nūntiāvit, ad tabernam festīnāvit.
   c   rēx, postquam gladiātōrī pecūniam dedit, leōnem mortuum īnspexit.

4   You have now met sentences with **quamquam** and **simulac**.
Study the following examples:

   a   Pompēius custōdēs interfēcit.
   Pompeius killed the guards.
   Pompēius, quamquam invītus erat, custōdēs interfēcit.
   Pompeius, although he was unwilling, killed the guards.

   Or, in more natural English:
   Although Pompeius was unwilling, he killed the guards.

   b   puer ē triclīniō contendit.
   The boy hurried out of the dining-room.

   simulac Salvius signum dedit, puer ē triclīniō contendit.
   As soon as Salvius gave the signal, the boy hurried out of the dining-room.

5   Further examples:

    a   coquus fūrem cōnspexit.
        coquus, simulac vīllam intrāvit, fūrem cōnspexit.

    b   Salvius nōn erat contentus.
        Salvius, quamquam servī dīligenter labōrābant, nōn erat contentus.

    c   Quīntus 'ecce!' clāmāvit.
        simulac nāvem vīdit, Quīntus 'ecce!' clāmāvit.

    d   nūntius ad templum cucurrit.
        nūntius, quamquam fessus erat, ad templum cucurrit.

6   The following examples are different types of longer sentences.
    Translate them.

    a   amīcī, simulac tabernam vīdērunt dīreptam, ad Clēmentem cucurrērunt.
    b   ubi Salvius revēnit īrātus, Bregāns fūgit.
    c   imperātor, postquam gladiātōribus lībertātem dedit, ex amphitheātrō exiit.
    d   Clēmēns, quod Eutychus tabernae iam appropinquābat, amīcōs arcessīvit.

7   Complete each sentence with the most suitable group of words
    from the box below, and then translate. Use each group of words
    once only.

> ubi saxō appropinquant
> quamquam ancilla dīligenter labōrābat
> simulac sacerdōtēs ē cellā templī prōcessērunt
> postquam hospitī cubiculum ostendit
> ubi iuvenēs laetī ad theātrum contendērunt
> quod turbam īnfestam audīre poterat

    a   . . . ., domina nōn erat contenta.
    b   necesse est nautīs, ..., cursum tenēre rēctum.
    c   puer timēbat ē casā exīre, ...
    d   . . . ., tacuērunt omnēs.
    e   māter, ..., cibum in culīnā gustāvit.
    f   . . . ., senex in tablīnō manēbat occupātus.

Longer sentences II

1   You have met several examples of this kind of sentence:

   Rēgnēnsēs erant laetī, Canticī miserī.
   The Regnenses were happy, the Cantici were miserable.

   Britannī cibum laudāvērunt, Rōmānī vīnum.
   The Britons praised the food, the Romans praised the wine.

2   Further examples:

   a   ūnus servus est fūr, cēterī innocentēs.
   b   Canticī Belimicum spectābant, Rēgnēnsēs Dumnorigem.

3   The following examples are slightly different:

   sacerdōs templum, poēta tabernam quaerēbat.
   The priest was looking for a temple, the poet was looking for an inn.

   iuvenis Aegyptius, senex Graecus erat.
   The young man was Egyptian, the old man was Greek.

4   Further examples:

   a   Clēmēns attonitus, Quīntus īrātus erat.
   b   mercātor stolās, caupō vīnum vēndēbat.
   c   puer ad hortum, ancillae ad ātrium ruērunt.
   d   Galatēa deam, iuvenēs Helenam spectābant.

Part Two: Vocabulary

1   Nouns are listed in the following way:

the nominative case, e.g. **servus** (*slave*);
the genitive case, e.g. **servī** (*of a slave*); this is explained in Stage 17;
the gender of the noun (m. = masculine, f. = feminine, n. = neuter);
this is explained in Stage 18.

So, if the following forms are given:
pāx, pācis, f.   *peace*
pāx means *peace*, **pācis** means *of peace*, and the word is feminine.

2   Find the meaning of the following.

    a   umerus, umerī
    b   seges, segetis
    c   scapha, scaphae

3   Find the meaning and the gender of the following words, some of which are in the nominative case and some in the genitive.

    a   taurus   **d**   tempestātis
    b   flūminis   **e**   dolor
    c   hastae   **f**   praediī

4   Using both **About the language** pp.150–1 and the **Vocabulary**, translate the following.

    a   leō; servō
    b   cīvī; dominī
    c   flōris; fabrīs
    d   amīcī; iuvenī

5   Adjectives are listed in the following way:

1st and 2nd declension adjectives are listed with the masculine, feminine and neuter forms of the nominative singular, e.g. **bonus, bona, bonum**.

3rd declension adjectives are usually given in the nominative masculine singular, e.g. **fortis, tristis**. Sometimes the genitive singular (which is the same for all genders) is added, e.g. **ferōx**, *gen.* **ferōcis**; **ingēns**, *gen.* **ingentis**.

6 Verbs are usually listed in the following way:

parō, parāre, parāvī   *prepare*

The first form listed (**parō**) is the 1st person singular of the present tense (*I prepare*).
The second form (**parāre**) is the infinitive (*to prepare*).
The third form (**parāvī**) is the 1st person singular of the perfect tense (*I prepared*).

So, if the following forms are given:

āmittō, āmittere, āmīsī   *lose*

āmittō means *I lose*, **āmittere** means *to lose*, **āmīsī** means *I lost*.

7 Find the meaning of the following.

  a   susurrō; susurrāre; susurrāvī.
  b   agō; agere; ēgī.
  c   haereō; impedīre; importāvī; vibrāre; interfēcī.

8 Find the meaning of the following.

a	tenēmus; tenuimus	**d**	quaesīvistī; quaerēbās
b	circumspectāvērunt; circumspectant	**e**	mittit; mīsit
c	tangō; tetigī	**f**	faciēbātis; fēcistī

9 All words which are given in the **Vocabulary checklists** for Stages 1–20 are marked with an asterisk(*).

a

* ā, ab	*from; by*
* abeō, abīre, abiī	*go away*
abiciō, abicere, abiēcī	*throw away*
* absum, abesse, āfuī	*be out, be absent*
accidō, accidere, accidī	*happen*
* accipiō, accipere, accēpī	*accept, take in, receive*
accurrēns, *gen.* accurrentis	*running up*
acētum, acētī, n.	*vinegar*
* ad	*to, at*
* adeō, adīre, adiī	*approach, go up to*
adeō	*so much, so greatly*
adest *see* adsum	
adiuvō, adiuvāre, adiūvī	*help*
administrāns, *gen.* administrantis	*looking after, managing*
administrō, administrāre, administrāvī	*look after, manage*
admittō, admittere, admīsī	*admit, let in*
adōrō, adōrāre, adōrāvī	*worship*
* adsum, adesse, adfuī	*be here, be present*
adveniēns, *gen.* advenientis	*arriving*
* adveniō, advenīre, advēnī	*arrive*
* aedificium, aedificiī, n.	*building*
* aedificō, aedificāre, aedificāvī	*build*
* aeger, aegra, aegrum	*sick, ill*
Aegyptius, Aegyptia, Aegyptium	*Egyptian*
Aegyptus, Aegyptī, f.	*Egypt*
aēneus, aēnea, aēneum	*made of bronze*
Aethiopes, Aethiopum, m.pl.	*Ethiopians*
afflīgō, afflīgere, afflīxī	*afflict, hurt*
ager, agrī, m.	*field*
agilis	*agile, nimble*
* agitō, agitāre, agitāvī	*chase, hunt*
* agmen, agminis, n.	*column (of men), procession*
* agnōscō, agnōscere, agnōvī	*recognise*
agnus, agnī, m.	*lamb*
* agō, agere, ēgī	*do, act*
age!	*come on!*
* grātiās agere	*thank, give thanks*
negōtium agere	*do business, work*
quid agis?	*how are you?*
* agricola, agricolae, m.	*farmer*
Alexandrīnus, Alexandrīna, Alexandrīnum	*Alexandrian*
aliquandō	*sometimes*
* aliquid	*something*
* alius, alia, aliud	*other, another, else*
* alter, altera, alterum	*the other, the second*
ambulāns, *gen.* ambulantis	*walking*
* ambulō, ambulāre, ambulāvī	*walk*
amīca, amīcae, f.	*friend (female)*
amīcē	*in a friendly way*
* amīcus, amīcī, m.	*friend (male)*
* āmittō, āmittere, āmīsī	*lose*
* amō, amāre, amāvī	*love, like*
amphora, amphorae, f.	*wine-jar*
amulētum, amulētī, n.	*amulet, lucky charm*
* ancilla, ancillae, f.	*slave-girl, maid*
animal, animālis, n.	*animal*
* animus, animī, m.	*spirit, soul, mind*
animum recipere	*recover consciousness*
anteā	*before*
antīquus, antīqua, antīquum	*old, ancient*
* ānulus, ānulī, m.	*ring*
anus, anūs, f.	*old woman*
anxius, anxia, anxium	*anxious*
aperiō, aperīre, aperuī	*open*
appāreō, appārēre, appāruī	*appear*
* appropinquō, appropinquāre, appropinquāvī	*approach, come near to*
* apud	*among, at the house of*
* aqua, aquae, f.	*water*
aquila, aquilae, f.	*eagle*
* āra, ārae, f.	*altar*
arānea, arāneae, f.	*spider's web*
arātor, arātōris, m.	*ploughman*
arca, arcae, f.	*strong-box, chest*
* arcessō, arcessere, arcessīvī	*summon, send for*
ardeō, ardēre, arsī	*burn, be on fire*
ārea, āreae, f.	*courtyard*
argenteus, argentea, argenteum	*made of silver*
armārium, armāriī, n.	*chest, cupboard*
* ars, artis, f.	*art, skill*
ascendō, ascendere, ascendī	*climb, rise*
asinus, asinī, m.	*ass, donkey*
assiduē	*continually*
astrologus, astrologī, m.	*astrologer*
Athēnae, Athēnārum, f.pl.	*Athens*
Athēniēnsis	*Athenian*
āthlēta, āthlētae, m.	*athlete*
ātrium, ātriī, n.	*atrium, main room, hall*
* attonitus, attonita, attonitum	*astonished*
* audeō, audēre	*dare*
* audiō, audīre, audīvī	*hear, listen to*
* aula, aulae, f.	*palace*
aurātus, aurāta, aurātum	*gilded, gold-plated*
aureus, aurea, aureum	*golden, made of gold*
aureus, aureī, m.	*gold coin*
auris, auris, f.	*ear*
* auxilium, auxiliī, n.	*help*
avārus, avāra, avārum	*mean, miserly*
avārus, avārī, m.	*miser*
avidus, avida, avidum	*eager*

b

bālō, bālāre, bālāvī	bleat
* bene	well
* benignus, benigna, benignum	kind
bēstia, bēstiae, f.	wild beast
* bibō, bibere, bibī	drink
* bonus, bona, bonum	good
Britannī, Britannōrum, m.pl.	Britons
Britannia, Britanniae, f.	Britain
Britannicus, Britannica, Britannicum	British

c

cachinnāns, gen. cachinnantis	laughing, cackling
cachinnō, cachinnāre, cachinnāvī	laugh, cackle, roar with laughter
cachinnus, cachinnī, m.	laughter
caedō, caedere, cecīdī	kill
caerimōnia, caerimōniae, f.	ceremony
calcō, calcāre, calcāvī	tread on
* callidus, callida, callidum	clever, cunning
candēlābrum, candēlābrī, n.	lamp-stand, candelabrum
* canis, canis, m.	dog
canistrum, canistrī, n.	basket
cantāns, gen. cantantis	singing
* cantō, cantāre, cantāvī	sing, chant
capillī, capillōrum, m.pl.	hair
* capiō, capere, cēpī	take, catch, capture
cōnsilium capere	make a plan, have an idea
captus, capta, captum	taken, caught, captured
* caput, capitis, n.	head
carnifex, carnificis, m.	executioner
* cārus, cāra, cārum	dear
casa, casae, f.	small house
caudex, caudicis, m.	blockhead, idiot
caupō, caupōnis, m.	innkeeper
cautē	cautiously
cecīdī see caedō	
cēdō, cēdere, cessī	give in, give way
celebrō, celebrāre, celebrāvī	celebrate
* celeriter	quickly
celerrimē	very quickly
quam celerrimē	as quickly as possible
cella, cellae, f.	sanctuary
cellārius, cellāriī, m.	steward
* cēna, cēnae, f.	dinner
* cēnō, cēnāre, cēnāvī	dine, have dinner
centum	a hundred

cēpī see capiō	
cēra, cērae, f.	wax, wax tablet
cērātus, cērāta, cērātum	wax, made of wax
certāmen, certāminis, n.	struggle, contest
certāmen nāvāle	boat-race
certō, certāre, certāvī	compete
certus, certa, certum	certain, infallible
cessī see cēdō	
* cēterī, cēterae, cētera	the others, the rest
* cibus, cibī, m.	food
circum	around
* circumspectō, circumspectāre, circumspectāvī	look round
circumveniō, circumvenīre, circumvēnī	surround
citharoedus, citharoedī, m.	cithara player
* cīvis, cīvis, m. f.	citizen
clādēs, clādis, f.	disaster
clam	secretly, in private
clāmāns, gen. clāmantis	shouting
* clāmō, clāmāre, clāmāvī	shout
* clāmor, clāmōris, m.	shout, uproar
claudicō, claudicāre, claudicāvī	be lame, limp
* claudō, claudere, clausī	shut, close, block
* coepī	I began
* cōgitō, cōgitāre, cōgitāvī	think, consider
* cognōscō, cognōscere, cognōvī	get to know, find out
collēctus, collēcta, collēctum	gathered, assembled
colligō, colligere, collēgī	gather, collect, assemble
collocō, collocāre, collocāvī	place, put
columba, columbae, f.	dove
cōmis	polite, courteous, friendly
cōmiter	politely, courteously
commemorō, commemorāre, commemorāvī	talk about
* commodus, commoda, commodum	convenient
commōtus, commōta, commōtum	moved, alarmed, excited, distressed
* comparō, comparāre, comparāvī	obtain
competītor, competītōris, m.	competitor
* compleō, complēre, complēvī	fill
compōnō, compōnere, composuī	put together, arrange, mix, make up
condūcō, condūcere, condūxī	hire
cōnfectus, cōnfecta, cōnfectum	finished
* cōnficiō, cōnficere, cōnfēcī	finish
cōnfīdō, cōnfīdere	trust
coniciō, conicere, coniēcī	hurl, throw

coniungō, coniungere,
  coniūnxī   *join*
  sē coniungere   *join*
coniūrātiō,
  coniūrātiōnis, f.   *plot, conspiracy*
coniūrō, coniūrāre,
  coniūrāvī   *plot, conspire*
cōnscendō, cōnscendere,
  cōnscendī   *embark on, go on board*
cōnscius, cōnsciī, m.   *accomplice*
cōnsecrō, cōnsecrāre,
  cōnsecrāvī   *dedicate*
* cōnsentiō, cōnsentīre,
  cōnsēnsī   *agree*
cōnserō, cōnserere,
  cōnseruī   *stitch*
cōnsīdō, cōnsīdere,
  cōnsēdī   *sit down*
* cōnsilium, cōnsiliī, n. *plan, idea*
  cōnsilium capere   *make a plan, have an idea*
cōnsistō, cōnsistere,
  cōnstitī   *stand one's ground, stand firm*
* cōnspiciō, cōnspicere,
  cōnspexī   *catch sight of*
* cōnsūmō, cōnsūmere,
  cōnsūmpsī   *eat*
* contendō, contendere,
  contendī   *hurry*
contentiō, contentiōnis, f. *argument*
* contentus, contenta,
  contentum   *satisfied*
contrōversia,
  contrōversiae, f.   *debate*
* conveniō, convenīre,
  convēnī   *come together, gather, meet*
convertō, convertere,
  convertī   *turn*
  sē convertere   *turn*
* coquō, coquere, coxī *cook*
* coquus, coquī, m.   *cook*
corōna, corōnae, f.   *garland, wreath*
* cotīdiē   *every day*
* crēdō, crēdere, crēdidī *trust, believe, have faith in*
crīnēs, crīnium, m.pl.   *hair*
crocodīlus, crocodīlī, m. *crocodile*
* crūdēlis   *cruel*
* cubiculum, cubiculī, n. *bedroom*
cucurrī *see* currō
culīna, culīnae, f.   *kitchen*
* cum   *with*
* cupiō, cupere, cupīvī *want*
* cūr?   *why?*
cūra, cūrae, f.   *care*
* cūrō, cūrāre, cūrāvī *look after, supervise*
  nihil cūrō   *I don't care*
currēns, *gen.* currentis *running*
* currō, currere, cucurrī *run*
cursus, cursūs, m.   *course*
* custōdiō, custōdīre,
  custōdīvī   *guard*

* custōs, custōdis, m.   *guard*
cutis, cutis, f.   *skin*

—————— d ——————

dare *see* dō
* dē   *from, down from; about*
* dea, deae, f.   *goddess*
* dēbeō, dēbēre, dēbuī *owe, ought, should, must*
* decem   *ten*
dēcidō, dēcidere, dēcidī *fall down*
dēcipiō, dēcipere, dēcēpī *deceive, fool*
* decōrus, decōra, decōrum *right, proper*
dedī *see* dō
dēfendēns,
  gen. dēfendentis   *defending*
dēfendō, dēfendere,
  dēfendī   *defend*
dēiciō, dēicere, dēiēcī *throw down, throw*
* deinde   *then*
* dēlectō, dēlectāre,
  dēlectāvī   *delight, please*
* dēleō, dēlēre, dēlēvī *destroy*
dēliciae, dēliciārum, f.pl. *darling*
dēligātus, dēligāta,
  dēligātum   *tied up, moored*
dēligō, dēligāre, dēligāvī *bind, tie, tie up*
* dēmōnstrō, dēmōnstrāre,
  dēmōnstrāvī   *point out, show*
dēnārius, dēnāriī, m. *a denarius (coin)*
* dēnique   *at last, finally*
dēpellō, dēpellere, dēpulī *drive off*
dēplōrāns,
  gen. dēplōrantis   *complaining about*
dēplōrō, dēplōrāre,
  dēplōrāvī   *complain about*
dērīdeō, dērīdēre, dērīsī *mock, jeer at*
dēscendō, dēscendere,
  dēscendī   *come down*
dēserō, dēserere, dēseruī *desert*
dēsertus, dēserta,
  dēsertum   *deserted*
  in dēsertīs   *in the desert*
dēsiliō, dēsilīre, dēsiluī *jump down*
dēspērāns,
  gen. dēspērantis   *despairing*
* dēspērō, dēspērāre,
  dēspērāvī   *despair*
dēstringō, dēstringere,
  dēstrīnxī   *draw out*
* deus, deī, m.   *god*
dexter, dextra, dextrum *right*
  ad dextram   *to the right*
diadēma, diadēmatis, n. *diadem, crown*
* dīcō, dīcere, dīxī   *say*
dictō, dictāre, dictāvī *dictate*
* diēs, diēī, m.   *day*

diēs fēstus, diēī fēstī, m.	*festival, holiday*
* difficilis	*difficult*
dignitās, dignitātis, f.	*dignity*
* dīligenter	*carefully*
dīmittō, dīmittere, dīmīsī	*send away, dismiss*
dīreptus, dīrepta, dīreptum	*pulled apart, ransacked*
dīrigō, dīrigere, dīrēxī	*steer*
dīripiō, dīripere, dīripuī	*pull apart, ransack*
dīrus, dīra, dīrum	*dreadful*
discēdēns, *gen.* discēdentis	*leaving, departing*
* discēdō, discēdere, discessī	*depart, leave*
discus, discī, m.	*discus*
dissecō, dissecāre, dissecuī	*cut up*
dissectus, dissecta, dissectum	*cut up, dismembered*
* diū	*for a long time*
diūtius	*any longer*
dīves, *gen.* dīvitis	*rich*
dīxī *see* dīcō	
* dō, dare, dedī	*give*
doceō, docēre, docuī	*teach*
* doctus, docta, doctum	*learned, educated, skilful, clever*
dolor, dolōris, m.	*pain*
* domina, dominae, f.	*mistress, madam*
* dominus, dominī, m.	*master*
* domus, domūs, f.	*home*
domī	*at home*
domum redīre	*return home*
* dōnum, dōnī, n.	*present, gift*
* dormiō, dormīre, dormīvī	*sleep*
dubitō, dubitāre, dubitāvī	*be doubtful*
dubium, dubiī, n.	*doubt*
* dūcō, dūcere, dūxī	*lead, take*
dulcis	*sweet*
mī dulcissime!	*my dear fellow!*
* duo	*two*
dūrus, dūra, dūrum	*hard, harsh*

——— e ———

* ē, ex	*from, out of*
eam	*her, it*
eārum	*their*
eās	*them*
* ecce!	*see! look!*
effigiēs, effigiēī, f.	*image, statue*
effluō, effluere, efflūxī	*pour out, flow out*
effodiō, effodere, effōdī	*dig*
effringō, effringere, effrēgī	*break down*
* effugiō, effugere, effūgī	*escape*
effundō, effundere, effūdī	*pour out*

ēgī *see* agō	
* ego, meī	*I, me*
mēcum	*with me*
ehem!	*well, well!*
* ēheu!	*oh dear! oh no!*
eī	*to him, to her, to it*
eīs	*to them, for them*
eius	*his*
ēlegāns, *gen.* ēlegantis	*tasteful, elegant*
ēligō, ēligere, ēlēgī	*choose*
ēlūdō, ēlūdere, ēlūsī	*slip past*
* ēmittō, ēmittere, ēmīsī	*throw, send out*
* emō, emere, ēmī	*buy*
ēmoveō, ēmovēre, ēmōvī	*move, clear away*
enim	*for*
eō	*it*
* eō, īre, iī	*go*
eōrum	*their*
eōs	*them*
* epistula, epistulae, f.	*letter*
eques, equitis, m.	*horseman*
equitō, equitāre, equitāvī	*ride*
* equus, equī, m.	*horse*
eram *see* sum	
ērubēscēns, *gen.* ērubēscentis	*blushing*
ērumpō, ērumpere, ērūpī	*break away*
est *see* sum	
* et	*and*
* etiam	*even*
euge!	*hurray!*
* eum	*him, it*
ēvellēns, *gen.* ēvellentis	*wrenching off*
ēvertō, ēvertere, ēvertī	*overturn*
ēvolō, ēvolāre, ēvolāvī	*fly out*
ēvulsus, ēvulsa, ēvulsum	*wrenched off*
* ex, ē	*from, out of*
exanimātus, exanimāta, exanimātum	*unconscious*
* excitō, excitāre, excitāvī	*arouse, wake up*
exclāmāns, *gen.* exclāmantis	*exclaiming, shouting*
* exclāmō, exclāmāre, exclāmāvī	*exclaim, shout*
* exeō, exīre, exiī	*go out*
exerceō, exercēre, exercuī	*practise, exercise*
exercitus, exercitūs, m.	*army*
expellō, expellere, expulī	*throw out*
exquīsītus, exquīsīta, exquīsītum	*special*
exspectātus, exspectāta, exspectātum	*welcome*
* exspectō, exspectāre, exspectāvī	*wait for*
extendō, extendere, extendī	*stretch out*
extorqueō, extorquēre, extorsī	*extort*
extrā	*outside*
extrahō, extrahere, extrāxī	*pull out, take out*

f

* faber, fabrī, m. — *craftsman*
* fābula, fābulae, f. — *story, play*
* facile — *easily*
* facilis — *easy*
* faciō, facere, fēcī — *make, do*
  familiāris, familiāris, m. — *relation, relative*
  familiāriter — *closely, intimately*
* faveō, favēre, fāvī — *favour, support*
  fax, facis, f. — *torch*
  fēcī *see* faciō
  fēlēs, fēlis, f. — *cat*
* fēmina, fēminae, f. — *woman*
  fenestra, fenestrae, f. — *window*
* ferō, ferre, tulī — *bring, carry*
  graviter ferre — *take badly*
* ferōciter — *fiercely*
* ferōx, *gen.* ferōcis — *fierce, ferocious*
  ferrum, ferrī, n. — *iron*
  fervēns, *gen.* ferventis — *boiling*
* fessus, fessa, fessum — *tired*
* festīnō, festīnāre, festīnāvī — *hurry*
  fēstus, fēsta, fēstum — *festival, holiday*
* fidēlis — *faithful, loyal*
* fīlia, fīliae, f. — *daughter*
* fīlius, fīliī, m. — *son*
  firmē — *firmly*
* flamma, flammae, f. — *flame*
* flōs, flōris, m. — *flower*
  flūmen, flūminis, n. — *river*
* fluō, fluere, flūxī — *flow*
  foedus, foeda, foedum — *foul, filthy*
  fōns, fontis, m. — *fountain*
  forceps, forcipis, m. — *doctors' tongs, forceps*
* fortasse — *perhaps*
* forte — *by chance*
* fortis — *brave*
* fortiter — *bravely*
  fortitūdō, fortitūdinis, f. — *courage*
  fortūna, fortūnae, f. — *fortune, luck*
  fortūnāta, fortūnātum — *lucky*
  forum, forī, n. — *forum, market-place*
  fossa, fossae, f. — *ditch*
  frāctus, frācta, frāctum — *broken*
  frangēns, *gen.* frangentis — *breaking*
* frāter, frātris, m. — *brother*
  frequentō, frequentāre, frequentāvī — *crowd*
  frūmentum, frūmentī, n. — *grain*
* frūstrā — *in vain*
  fugiēns, *gen.* fugientis — *running away, fleeing*
* fugiō, fugere, fūgī — *run away, flee (from)*
  fuī *see* sum
  fundō, fundere, fūdī — *pour*
* fundus, fundī, m. — *farm*

* fūr, fūris, m. — *thief*
  furēns, *gen.* furentis — *furious, in a rage*
  fūstis, fūstis, m. — *club*

g

  garriēns, *gen.* garrientis — *chattering, gossiping*
  garriō, garrīre, garrīvī — *chatter, gossip*
  garum, garī, n. — *sauce*
  geminī, geminōrum, m.pl. — *twins*
  gemitus, gemitūs, m. — *groan*
  gēns, gentis, f. — *family, tribe*
  Germānicus, Germānica, Germānicum — *German*
  gerō, gerere, gessī — *wear*
  gladiātor, gladiātōris, m. — *gladiator*
* gladius, gladiī, m. — *sword*
  Graecia, Graeciae, f. — *Greece*
  Graecus, Graeca, Graecum — *Greek*
  grātiae, grātiārum, f.pl. — *thanks*
* grātiās agere — *give thanks, thank*
  gravis — *heavy*
* graviter — *seriously*
  graviter ferre — *take badly*
  gustō, gustāre, gustāvī — *taste*

h

* habeō, habēre, habuī — *have*
* habitō, habitāre, habitāvī — *live*
  hāc — *this*
  hae — *these*
  haec — *this*
  haedus, haedī, m. — *kid, young goat*
  haereō, haerēre, haesī — *stick, cling*
  hanc — *this*
  hās — *these*
* hasta, hastae, f. — *spear*
  hauriō, haurīre, hausī — *drain, drink up*
  hercle! — *by Hercules! good heavens!*
* herī — *yesterday*
  heus! — *hey!*
  hī — *these*
* hic — *this*
  hiemō, hiemāre, hiemāvī — *spend the winter*
  hiems, hiemis, f. — *winter*
  hippopotamus, hippopotamī, m. — *hippopotamus*
  hoc — *this*
  hōc — *this*
* hodiē — *today*
* homō, hominis, m. — *human being, man*

homunculus,
  homunculī, m.   *little man*
honōrō, honōrāre,
  honōrāvī   *honour*
hōra, hōrae, f.   *hour*
horreum, horreī, n.   *barn, granary*
* hortus, hortī, m.   *garden*
hōs   *these*
* hospes, hospitis, m.   *guest, host*
* hūc   *here, to this place*
humilis   *low-born, of low class*
hunc   *this*

i

iacēns, *gen.* iacentis   *lying*
* iaceō, iacēre, iacuī   *lie*
iactō, iactāre, iactāvī   *throw*
* iam   *now*
* iānua, iānuae, f.   *door*
ībam *see* eō
* ibi   *there*
id   *it*
* igitur   *therefore, and so*
* ignāvus, ignāva, ignāvum   *lazy, cowardly*
ignōrō, ignōrāre, ignōrāvī   *not know about*
illa   *that, she*
illā   *that*
illae   *those*
illam   *that*
illās   *those*
* ille   *that, he*
illī   *they, those, that*
illōs   *those*
* illūc   *there, to that place*
illud   *that*
illum   *that*
immemor,
  gen. immemoris   *forgetful*
immortālis   *immortal*
immōtus, immōta,
  immōtum   *still, motionless*
impavidus, impavida,
  impavidum   *fearless*
* impediō, impedīre,
  impedīvī   *delay, hinder*
impellō, impellere,
  impulī   *carry, push, force*
* imperātor,
  imperātōris, m.   *emperor*
* imperium, imperiī, n.   *empire*
impetus, impetūs, m.   *attack*
impiger, impigra,
  impigrum   *lively, energetic*
importō, importāre,
  importāvī   *import*

impulī *see* impellō
* in   *in, on; into, onto*
incendēns,
  gen. incendentis   *burning, setting on fire*
incitō, incitāre, incitāvī   *urge on, encourage*
incolumis   *safe*
incurrō, incurrere, incurrī   *run onto, collide*
inēlegāns, *gen.* inēlegantis   *unattractive*
īnfēlīx, *gen.* īnfēlīcis   *unlucky*
* īnferō, īnferre, intulī   *bring in, bring on*
  iniūriam īnferre   *do an injustice to, bring injury to*
  vim īnferre   *use force, violence*
īnfestus, īnfesta, īnfestum   *hostile*
īnfirmus, īnfirma,
  īnfirmum   *weak*
īnflō, īnflāre, īnflāvī   *blow*
ingenium, ingeniī, n.   *character*
* ingēns, *gen.* ingentis   *huge*
ingravēscō, ingravēscere   *grow worse*
iniciō, inicere, iniēcī   *throw in*
inimīcus, inimīcī, m.   *enemy*
iniūria, iniūriae, f.   *injustice, injury*
iniūstē   *unfairly*
innocēns, *gen.* innocentis   *innocent*
* inquit   *says, said*
īnsānus, īnsāna, īnsānum   *mad, crazy*
īnsiliō, īnsilīre, īnsiluī   *jump onto, jump into*
īnsolēns, *gen.* īnsolentis   *rude, insolent*
* īnspiciō, īnspicere,
  īnspexī   *look at, inspect, examine*
īnstruō, īnstruere, īnstrūxī   *draw up*
  sē īnstruere   *draw oneself up*
* īnsula, īnsulae, f.   *island*
* intellegō, intellegere,
  intellēxī   *understand*
* intentē   *closely, carefully*
* inter   *among, between*
  inter sē   *among themselves, with each other*
intereā   *meanwhile*
* interficiō, interficere,
  interfēcī   *kill*
interpellō, interpellāre,
  interpellāvī   *interrupt*
interrogō, interrogāre,
  interrogāvī   *question*
* intrō, intrāre, intrāvī   *enter*
intulī *see* īnferō
inūtilis   *useless*
* inveniō, invenīre, invēnī   *find*
* invītō, invītāre, invītāvī   *invite*
* invītus, invīta, invītum   *unwilling, reluctant*
iocus, iocī, m.   *joke*
* ipsa   *herself*
* ipse   *himself*
* īrātus, īrāta, īrātum   *angry*
īre *see* eō
irrumpō, irrumpere,
  irrūpī   *burst in*
Īsiacus, Īsiacī, m.   *follower of Isis*

ista	*that*
istam	*that*
* iste	*that*
istum	*that*
* ita	*in this way*
ita vērō	*yes*
Ītalia, Ītaliae, f.	*Italy*
* itaque	*and so*
* iter, itineris, n.	*journey, progress*
* iterum	*again*
Iūdaeī, Iūdaeōrum, m.pl	*Jews*
* iūdex, iūdicis, m.	*judge*
* iuvenis, iuvenis, m.	*young man*

l

labōrāns, *gen.* labōrantis	*working*
* labōrō, labōrāre, labōrāvī	*work*
lacrima, lacrimae, f.	*tear*
lacrimīs sē trādere	*burst into tears*
lacrimāns,	
gen. lacrimantis	*weeping, crying*
* lacrimō, lacrimāre,	
lacrimāvī	*weep, cry*
laedō, laedere, laesī	*harm*
* laetus, laeta, laetum	*happy*
languidus, languida,	
languidum	*weak, feeble*
lateō, latēre, latuī	*lie hidden*
latrō, latrōnis, m.	*robber, thug*
* laudō, laudāre, laudāvī	*praise*
lavō, lavāre, lāvī	*wash*
* lectus, lectī, m.	*couch, bed*
* legō, legere, lēgī	*read*
lēniter	*gently*
* lentē	*slowly*
* leō, leōnis, m.	*lion*
levis	*changeable, inconsistent*
libellus, libellī, m.	*little book*
* libenter	*gladly*
* liber, librī, m.	*book*
* līberālis	*generous*
* līberō, līberāre, līberāvī	*free, set free*
* lībertus, lībertī, m.	*freedman, ex-slave*
lībō, lībāre, lībāvī	*pour an offering*
liquō, liquāre, liquāvī	*melt*
* lītus, lītoris, n.	*sea-shore, shore*
* locus, locī, m.	*place*
Londinium, Londiniī, n.	*London*
longē	*far, a long way*
longius	*further*
longus, longa, longum	*long*
loquāx, *gen.* loquācis	*talkative*
lūdus, lūdī, m.	*game*
lūdī fūnebrēs	*funeral games*
* lūna, lūnae, f.	*moon*

m

madidus, madida,	
madidum	*soaked through*
magicus, magica,	
magicum	*magic*
magis	*more*
multō magis	*much more*
magister, magistrī, m.	*foreman*
magnificus, magnifica,	
magnificum	*splendid, magnificent*
* magnus, magna, magnum	*big, large, great*
maior, *gen.* maiōris	*bigger, larger, greater*
* māne	*in the morning*
* maneō, manēre, mānsī	*remain, stay*
mānsuētus, mānsuēta,	
mānsuētum	*tame*
* manus, manūs, f.	*hand*
* mare, maris, n.	*sea*
* marītus, marītī, m.	*husband*
marmoreus, marmorea,	
marmoreum	*made of marble*
* māter, mātris, f.	*mother*
mātrōna, mātrōnae, f.	*lady*
maximē	*most of all, very much*
* maximus, maxima,	
maximum	*very big, very large, very great*
mē *see* ego	
medicāmentum,	
medicāmentī, n.	*ointment*
medicīna, medicīnae, f.	*medicine*
medicus, medicī, m.	*doctor*
* medius, media, medium	*middle*
mel, mellis, n.	*honey*
* melior	*better*
melius est	*it would be better*
mendācior,	
gen. mendāciōris	*more deceitful*
* mendāx, mendācis, m.	*liar*
mēnsa, mēnsae, f.	*table*
mēnsis, mēnsis, m.	*month*
* mercātor, mercātōris, m.	*merchant*
mēta, mētae, f.	*turning-point*
metallum, metallī, n.	*a mine*
* meus, mea, meum	*my, mine*
mī dulcissime!	*my dear fellow!*
mī Salvī!	*my dear Salvius!*
mihi *see* ego	
* mīles, mīlitis, m.	*soldier*
mīlitō, mīlitāre, mīlitāvī	*be a soldier*
* minimē!	*no!*
* mīrābilis	*extraordinary, strange*
mīrāculum, mīrāculī, n.	*miracle*
* miser, misera, miserum	*miserable, wretched, sad*
o mē miserum!	*oh wretched me! oh dear!*
* mittō, mittere, mīsī	*send*
modicus, modica,	
modicum	*ordinary, little*

molestus, molesta,
  molestum   *troublesome*
moneō, monēre, monuī   *warn, advise*
* mōns, montis, m.   *mountain*
monumentum,
  monumentī, n.   *monument*
moritūrus, moritūra,
  moritūrum   *going to die*
* mors, mortis, f.   *death*
* mortuus, mortua,
  mortuum   *dead*
moveō, movēre, mōvī   *move*
* mox   *soon*
mulceō, mulcēre, mulsī   *stroke*
multitūdō,
  multitūdinis, f.   *crowd*
* multus, multa, multum   *much*
*   multī   *many*
  multō magis   *much more*
* mūrus, mūrī, m.   *wall*
mūs, mūris, m. f.   *mouse*
mystēria, mystēriōrum,
  n.pl.   *mysteries, secret worship*

─────── **n** ───────

* nam   *for*
* nārrō, nārrāre, nārrāvī   *tell, relate*
natō, natāre, natāvī   *swim*
nātūra, nātūrae, f.   *nature*
naufragium, naufragiī, n.   *shipwreck*
naufragus, naufragī, m.   *shipwrecked sailor*
* nauta, nautae, m.   *sailor*
* nāvigō, nāvigāre,
  nāvigāvī   *sail*
* nāvis, nāvis, f.   *ship*
Neāpolis, Neāpolis, f.   *Naples*
* necesse   *necessary*
* necō, necāre, necāvī   *kill*
nefāstus, nefāsta,
  nefāstum   *dreadful*
neglegēns,
  gen. neglegentis   *careless*
* negōtium, negōtiī, n.   *business*
* nēmō   *no one, nobody*
neque… neque   *neither… nor*
niger, nigra, nigrum   *black*
* nihil   *nothing*
  nihil cūrō   *I don't care*
Nīlus, Nīlī, m.   *the river Nile*
nitidus, nitida, nitidum   *gleaming, brilliant*
niveus, nivea, niveum   *snow-white*
nōbilis   *noble, of noble birth*
nōbīs *see* nōs
nocēns, *gen.* nocentis   *guilty*
noceō, nocēre, nocuī   *hurt*

noctū   *by night*
* nōlō, nōlle, nōluī   *not want*
  nōlī   *do not, don't*
nōmen, nōminis, n.   *name*
* nōn   *not*
* nōnne?   *surely?*
nōnnūllī, nōnnūllae   *some, several*
* nōs   *we, us*
  nōbīscum   *with us*
* noster, nostra, nostrum   *our*
nōtus, nōta, nōtum   *well-known, famous*
* novem   *nine*
* nōvī   *I know*
* novus, nova, novum   *new*
* nūllus, nūlla, nūllum   *not any, no*
* num?   *surely not?*
numerō, numerāre,
  numerāvī   *count*
numerus, numerī, m.   *number*
* numquam   *never*
* nunc   *now*
* nūntiō, nūntiāre, nūntiāvī   *announce*
* nūntius, nūntiī, m.   *messenger, news*
nūper   *recently*
nūptiae, nūptiārum, f.pl.   *wedding*

─────── **o** ───────

obdormiō, obdormīre,
  obdormīvī   *go to sleep*
obeō, obīre, obiī   *meet*
obruō, obruere, obruī   *overwhelm*
obstinātus, obstināta,
  obstinātum   *obstinate, stubborn*
* obstō, obstāre, obstitī   *obstruct, block the way*
obtulī *see* offerō
occupātus, occupāta,
  occupātum   *busy*
* octō   *eight*
* oculus, oculī, m.   *eye*
offendō, offendere,
  offendī   *displease*
* offerō, offerre, obtulī   *offer*
officīna, officīnae, f.   *workshop*
* ōlim   *once, some time ago*
* omnis   *all*
opportūnē   *just at the right time*
oppugnō, oppugnāre,
  oppugnāvī   *attack*
* optimē   *very well*
* optimus, optima,
  optimum   *very good, excellent, best*
ōrdō, ōrdinis, m.   *row, line*
ōrnāmentum,
  ōrnāmentī, n.   *ornament*
ōrnātrīx, ōrnātrīcis, f.   *hairdresser*
ōrnātus, ōrnāta, ōrnātum   *decorated, elaborately furnished*

ōrnō, ōrnāre, ōrnāvī decorate
ōsculum, ōsculī, n. kiss
* ostendō, ostendere,
  ostendī show
ostrea, ostreae, f. oyster
ōtiōsus, ōtiōsa, ōtiōsum idle, on holiday, on vacation
ōvum, ōvī, n. egg

p

* paene nearly, almost
palaestra, palaestrae, f. palaestra, exercise area
palūs, palūdis, f. marsh, swamp
parātus, parāta, parātum ready, prepared
parēns, parentis, m. f. parent
pāreō, pārēre, pāruī obey
* parō, parāre, parāvī prepare
* pars, partis, f. part
  in prīmā parte in the forefront
* parvus, parva, parvum small, little
* pater, patris, m. father
patera, paterae, f. bowl
* paucī, paucae few, a few
paulātim gradually
paulum, paulī, n. little, a little
pavīmentum,
  pavīmentī, n. floor
* pāx, pācis, f. peace
* pecūnia, pecūniae, f. money
* per through, along
percutiō, percutere,
  percussī strike
* pereō, perīre, periī die, perish
perīculōsus, perīculōsa,
  perīculōsum dangerous
* perīculum, perīculī, n. danger
perītē skilfully
perītia, perītiae, f. skill
perītus, perīta, perītum skilful
* persuādeō, persuādēre,
  persuāsī persuade
* perterritus, perterrita,
  perterritum terrified
* perveniō, pervenīre,
  pervēnī reach, arrive at
* pēs, pedis, m. foot, paw
* pessimus, pessima,
  pessimum worst, very bad
pestis, pestis, f. pest, scoundrel
* petō, petere, petīvī make for, attack; seek, beg for, ask
  for
pharus, pharī, m. lighthouse
philosophus,
  philosophī, m. philosopher
pictor, pictōris, m. painter, artist
pictūra, pictūrae, f. painting, picture

pila, pilae, f. ball
pingō, pingere, pīnxī paint
pius, pia, pium respectful to the gods
* placeō, placēre, placuī please, suit
placidus, placida,
  placidum calm, peaceful
plānē clearly
* plaudō, plaudere,
  plausī applaud, clap
plaustrum, plaustrī, n. wagon, cart
plēnus, plēna, plēnum full
pluit, pluere, pluit rain
* plūrimus, plūrima,
  plūrimum most, very much
* plūrimī, plūrimae very many
poena, poenae, f. punishment
  poenās dare pay the penalty, be punished
* poēta, poētae, m. poet
pompa, pompae, f. procession
Pompēiānus, Pompēiāna,
  Pompēiānum Pompeian
* pōnō, pōnere, posuī place, put, put up
* porta, portae, f. gate
portāns, gen. portantis carrying
* portō, portāre, portāvī carry
* portus, portūs, m. harbour
* poscō, poscere, poposcī demand, ask for
possideō, possidēre,
  possēdī possess
* possum, posse, potuī can, be able
* post after, behind
* posteā afterwards
* postquam after, when
postrēmō finally, lastly
* postrīdiē on the next day
* postulō, postulāre,
  postulāvī demand
posuī see pōnō
potuī see possum
praeceps, gen. praecipitis headlong
praecursor,
  praecursōris, m. forerunner
praedium, praediī, n. estate
praemium, praemiī, n. prize, reward, profit
praesidium, praesidiī, n. protection
praesum, praeesse,
  praefuī be in charge of
praetereō, praeterīre,
  praeteriī go past
prāvus, prāva, prāvum evil
precēs, precum, f.pl. prayers
premō, premere, pressī push
pretiōsus, pretiōsa,
  pretiōsum expensive, precious
pretium, pretiī, n. price
prīmō first
* prīmus, prīma, prīmum first
  in prīmā parte in the forefront
* prīnceps, prīncipis, m. chief, chieftain
prior first, in front

* prō — *in front of*
  prō dī immortālēs! — *heavens above!*
probus, proba, probum — *honest*
* prōcēdō, prōcēdere,
  prōcessī — *advance, proceed*
procul — *far off*
prōcumbō, prōcumbere,
  prōcubuī — *fall, fall down*
* prōmittō, prōmittere,
  prōmīsī — *promise*
* prope — *near*
prōvideō, prōvidēre,
  prōvīdī — *foresee*
proximus, proxima,
  proximum — *nearest*
psittacus, psittacī, m. — *parrot*
* puella, puellae, f. — *girl*
* puer, puerī, m. — *boy*
pugiō, pugiōnis, m. — *dagger*
* pugna, pugnae, f. — *fight*
* pugnō, pugnāre, pugnāvī — *fight*
* pulcher, pulchra,
  pulchrum — *beautiful*
* pulsō, pulsāre, pulsāvī — *hit, knock at, punch*
pūmiliō, pūmiliōnis, m. — *dwarf*
* pūniō, pūnīre, pūnīvī — *punish*
pūrus, pūra, pūrum — *clean, spotless*
puto, putāre, putāvī — *think*

q

quā — *from whom*
* quadrāgintā — *forty*
quae — *who, which*
quaerēns, *gen.* quaerentis — *searching for, looking for*
* quaerō, quaerere,
  quaesīvī — *search for, look for*
* quam — *(1) how*
  quam celerrimē — *as quickly as possible*
* quam — *(2) than*
quam — *(3) whom, which*
* quamquam — *although*
quārtus, quārta, quārtum — *fourth*
quās — *whom, which*
* quattuor — *four*
* -que — *and*
quem — *whom, which*
* quī — *who, which*
quid? — *what?*
  quid agis? — *how are you?*
  quid vīs? — *what do you want?*
quīdam — *a certain*
quiēscō, quiēscere, quiēvī — *rest*
quiētus, quiēta, quiētum — *quiet*
* quīnquāgintā — *fifty*
* quīnque — *five*

* quis? — *who?*
* quō? — *(1) where? where to?*
quō — *(2) from whom*
quō modō? — *how?*
* quod — *(1) because*
quod — *(2) which*
* quondam — *one day, once*
* quoque — *also, too*
quōs — *whom, which*
quotannīs — *every year*

r

rādō, rādere, rāsī — *scratch*
rapiō, rapere, rapuī — *seize, grab*
rārō — *rarely*
raucus, rauca, raucum — *harsh*
recidō, recidere, reccidī — *fall back*
* recipiō, recipere, recēpī — *recover, take back*
  sē recipere — *recover*
recitāns, *gen.* recitantis — *reciting*
recitō, recitāre, recitāvī — *recite*
rēctā — *directly, straight*
rēctus, rēcta, rēctum — *straight*
recumbēns,
  gen. recumbentis — *lying down, reclining*
recumbō, recumbere,
  recubuī — *lie down, recline*
* recūsō, recūsāre, recūsāvī — *refuse*
* reddō, reddere, reddidī — *give back*
* redeō, redīre, rediī — *return, go back, come back*
referō, referre, rettulī — *carry, deliver*
reficiō, reficere, refēcī — *repair*
rēgīna, rēgīnae, f. — *queen*
* relinquō, relinquere,
  relīquī — *leave*
remedium, remediī, n. — *cure*
renovō, renovāre,
  renovāvī — *restore*
* rēs, reī, f. — *thing*
  rem cōnficere — *finish the job*
  rem intellegere — *understand the truth*
  rem nārrāre — *tell the story*
  rēs rūstica — *farming*
* resistō, resistere, restitī — *resist*
* respondeō, respondēre,
  respondī — *reply*
respōnsum, respōnsī, n. — *answer*
retineō, retinēre, retinuī — *keep, hold back*
retrahō, retrahere, retrāxī — *drag back*
* reveniō, revenīre, revēnī — *come back, return*
* rēx, rēgis, m. — *king*
rīdēns, *gen.* rīdentis — *laughing, smiling*
* rīdeō, rīdēre, rīsī — *laugh, smile*
rīpa, rīpae, f. — *river bank*
* rogō, rogāre, rogāvī — *ask*

rogus, rogī, m.	pyre
Rōmānus, Rōmāna, Rōmānum	Roman
rosa, rosae, f.	rose
rota, rotae, f.	wheel
* ruō, ruere, ruī	rush
rūsticus, rūstica, rūsticum	country, in the country
rēs rūstica	farming
vīlla rūstica	house in the country

—————— **S** ——————

sacer, sacra, sacrum	sacred
* sacerdōs, sacerdōtis, m.	priest
sacrificium, sacrificiī, n.	offering, sacrifice
sacrificō, sacrificāre, sacrificāvī	sacrifice
* saepe	often
saeviō, saevīre, saeviī	be in a rage
saevus, saeva, saevum	savage
saltātrīx, saltātrīcis, f.	dancing-girl
saltō, saltāre, saltāvī	dance
* salūtō, salūtāre, salūtāvī	greet
* salvē!	hello!
sānē	obviously
* sanguis, sanguinis, m.	blood
sānō, sānāre, sānāvī	heal, cure
sapiēns, gen. sapientis	wise
* satis	enough
saxum, saxī, n.	rock
scapha, scaphae, f.	punt, small boat
scelestus, scelesta, scelestum	wicked
scēptrum, scēptrī, n.	sceptre
scindō, scindere, scidī	tear, tear up
scio, scīre, scīvī	know
scōpae, scōpārum, f.pl.	broom
scopulus, scopulī, m.	reef
* scrībō, scrībere, scrīpsī	write
scrīptor, scrīptōris, m.	writer, sign-writer
scurrīlis	rude
* sē	himself, herself, themselves
sēcum	with him, with her, with them
secō, secāre, secuī	cut
secundus, secunda, secundum	second
sēcūrus, sēcūra, sēcūrum	without a care
* sed	but
sedēns, gen. sedentis	sitting
* sedeō, sedēre, sēdī	sit
seges, segetis, f.	crop, harvest
sella, sellae, f.	chair
sēmirutus, sēmiruta, sēmirutum	half-collapsed
* semper	always
* senātor, senātōris, m.	senator
* senex, senis, m.	old man

sententia, sententiae, f.	opinion
* sentiō, sentīre, sēnsī	feel, notice
* septem	seven
sermō, sermōnis, m.	conversation
* servō, servāre, servāvī	save, look after, preserve
* servus, servī, m.	slave
* sex	six
sibi	to him, to her, to them
* sīcut	like
* signum, signī, n.	sign, seal, signal
silentium, silentiī, n.	silence
* silva, silvae, f.	wood
* simulac, simulatque	as soon as
sine	without
situs, situs, m.	position, site
sōl, sōlis, m.	sun
* soleō, solēre	be accustomed
sollemniter	solemnly
sollicitūdō, sollicitūdinis, f.	anxiety
* sollicitus, sollicita, sollicitum	worried, anxious
* sōlus, sōla, sōlum	alone, lonely, only, on one's own
somnium, somniī, n.	dream
sonitus, sonitūs, m.	sound
sonō, sonāre, sonuī	sound
sonus, sonī, m.	sound, noise
sordidus, sordida, sordidum	dirty
spargō, spargere, sparsī	scatter
* spectāculum, spectāculī, n.	show, spectacle
spectātor, spectātōris, m.	spectator
* spectō, spectāre, spectāvī	look at, watch
splendidus, splendida, splendidum	splendid
spongia, spongiae, f.	sponge
stāns, gen. stantis	standing
* statim	at once
statua, statuae, f.	statue
stilus, stilī, m.	pen, stick
* stō, stāre, stetī	stand
stola, stolae, f.	dress
studeō, studēre, studuī	study
* stultus, stulta, stultum	stupid
suāvis	sweet
suāviter	sweetly
sub	under
* subitō	suddenly
sūdō, sūdāre, sūdāvī	sweat
sufficiō, sufficere, suffēcī	be enough
* sum, esse, fuī	be
summergō, summergere, summersī	sink, dip
summersus, summersa, summersum	sunk
* summus, summa, summum	highest, greatest, top
superbus, superba, superbum	arrogant, proud

* superō, superāre, superāvī		overcome, overpower
supersum, superesse, superfuī		survive
supplicium, suppliciī, n.		death penalty
surdus, surda, surdum		deaf
* surgō, surgere, surrēxī		get up, rise
suscipiō, suscipere, suscēpī		undertake, take on
sustulī see tollō		
susurrāns, gen. susurrantis		whispering, muttering
susurrō, susurrāre, susurrāvī		whisper, mutter
* suus, sua, suum		his, her, their, their own
Syrī, Syrōrum, m.pl		Syrians
Syrius, Syria, Syrium		Syrian

t

* taberna, tabernae, f.		shop, inn
tabernārius, tabernāriī, m.		shopkeeper
tablīnum, tablīnī, n.		study
* taceō, tacēre, tacuī		be silent, be quiet
* tacitē		quietly, silently
tacitus, tacita, tacitum		quiet, silent, in silence
* tam		so
* tamen		however
* tandem		at last
tangō, tangere, tetigī		touch
tantus, tanta, tantum		so great, such a great
tardus, tarda, tardum		late
taurus, taurī, m.		bull
tē see tū		
tempestās, tempestātis, f.		storm
* templum, templī, n.		temple
* temptō, temptāre, temptāvī		try
tenēns, gen. tenentis		holding
* teneō, tenēre, tenuī		hold
tergeō, tergēre, tersī		wipe
* terra, terrae, f.		ground, land
* terreō, terrēre, terruī		frighten
terribilis		terrible
theātrum, theātrī, n.		theatre
tibi see tū		
tībīcen, tībīcinis, m.		pipe player
* timeō, timēre, timuī		be afraid, fear
timidus, timida, timidum		fearful, frightened
toga, togae, f.		toga
tollēns, gen. tollentis		raising, lifting up
* tollō, tollere, sustulī		raise, lift up, hold up
* tot		so many
* tōtus, tōta, tōtum		whole
tractō, tractāre, tractāvī		handle
* trādō, trādere, trādidī		hand over

lacrimīs sē trādere		burst into tears
tragoedia, tragoediae, f.		tragedy
* trahō, trahere, trāxī		drag
tranquillitās, tranquillitātis, f.		calmness
trānsfīgō, trānsfīgere, trānsfīxī		pierce
* trēs		three
triclīnium, triclīniī, n.		dining-room
* trīgintā		thirty
tripodes, tripodum, m.pl.		tripods
trīstis		sad
trūdō, trūdere, trūsī		push, shove
* tū, tuī		you (singular)
tēcum		with you (singular)
tuba, tubae, f.		trumpet
tubicen, tubicinis, m.		trumpeter
tulī see ferō		
* tum		then
tumultus, tumultūs, m.		riot
tunica, tunicae, f.		tunic
* turba, turbae, f.		crowd
turbulentus, turbulenta, turbulentum		rowdy, disorderly
tūtus, tūta, tūtum		safe
tūtius est		it would be safer
* tuus, tua, tuum		your, yours

u

* ubi		where, when
ultor, ultōris, m.		avenger
umerus, umerī, m.		shoulder
* unda, undae, f.		wave
unde		from where
unguō, unguere, ūnxī		anoint, smear
* ūnus, ūna, ūnum		one
urbānus, urbāna, urbānum		smart, fashionable
* urbs, urbis, f.		city
urna, urnae, f.		bucket, jar, jug
ursa, ursae, f.		bear
ut		as
* uxor, uxōris, f.		wife

v

* valdē		very much, very
* valē		goodbye
valvae, valvārum, f.pl.		doors
varius, varia, varium		different
* vehementer		violently, loudly

vehō, vehere, vēxī — carry
vēnātiō, vēnātiōnis, f. — hunt
* vēndō, vēndere, vēndidī — sell
venia, veniae, f. — mercy
* veniō, venīre, vēnī — come
vēr, vēris, n. — spring
* verberō, verberāre,
    verberāvī — strike, beat
verrō, verrere — sweep
versus, versūs, m. — verse, line of poetry
    versus magicus — magic spell
* vertō, vertere, vertī — turn
    sē vertere — turn round
vērus, vēra, vērum — true, real
vester, vestra, vestrum — your (plural)
* vexō, vexāre, vexāvī — annoy
* via, viae, f. — street
vibrō, vibrāre, vibrāvī — wave, brandish
vīcī see vincō
vīcīnus, vīcīna; vīcīnum — neighbouring, nearby
victima, victimae, f. — victim
victor, victōris, m. — victor, winner
* videō, vidēre, vīdī — see
* vīgintī — twenty
vīlicus, vīlicī, m. — farm manager, bailiff
vīlis — cheap
vīlla, vīllae, f. — house, villa
* vincō, vincere, vīcī — win, be victorious
vindex, vindicis, m. — champion, defender
vindicō, vindicāre,
    vindicāvī — avenge
* vīnum, vīnī, n, — wine
* vir, virī, m. — man
virga, virgae, f. — rod, stick
vīs, f. — force, violence
vīs see volō
vīsitō, vīsitāre, vīsitāvī — visit
* vīta, vītae, f. — life
vītō, vītāre, vītāvī — avoid
vitreārius, vitreāriī, m. — glassmaker
vitreus, vitrea, vitreum — glass, made of glass
vitrum, vitrī, n. — glass
* vituperō, vituperāre,
    vituperāvī — blame, curse
* vīvō, vīvere, vīxī — live, be alive
* vix — hardly, scarcely, with difficulty
vōbīs see vōs
* vocō, vocāre, vocāvī — call
* volō, velle, voluī — want
    quid vīs? — what do you want?
* vōs — you (plural)
* vōx, vōcis, f. — voice
vulnerātus, vulnerāta,
    vulnerātum — wounded, injured
* vulnerō, vulnerāre,
    vulnerāvī — wound, injure
* vulnus, vulneris, n, — wound
vult see volō